FENG SHUI
GOES TO THE OFFICE

HOW TO
THRIVE FROM
9 TO 5

NANCILEE WYDRA

D0981745

CB
CONTEMPORARY BOOKS

Library of Congress Cataloging-in-Publication Data

Wydra, Nancilee.
    Feng shui goes to the office : how to thrive from 9 to 5 / Nancilee
Wydra.
      p.   cm.
    Includes index.
    ISBN 0-8092-2872-6
    1. Feng-shui.   2. Work environment—Psychological aspects.
    3. Job satisfaction.   I. Title.
BF1779.F4W935   2000
133.3′337—dc21

                                     99-33451
                                      CIP

Cover design by Jennifer Locke
Back cover photograph by Molly E. Freilicher
Interior design by Scott Rattray
Cover and interior illustrations by Ginny Piech Street

Published by Contemporary Books
A division of NTC/Contemporary Publishing Group, Inc.
4255 West Touhy Avenue, Lincolnwood (Chicago), Illinois 60712-1975 U.S.A.
Printed in the United States of America
International Standard Book Number: 0-8092-2872-6
00 01 02 03 04 LB 18 17 16 15 14 13 12 11 10 9 8 7 6 5 4 3 2 1

To ALL MY loved ones who have ever worked in an office, especially Sol Goodman, Gay Urso, Debra and Stuart Segal, Wendy, Michael, and Jonathan Sacks, Julie and Scott Kroll, Sandy and Tuv Vidan, Ben and Zac Wydra, and Sandy Sharrock, I wish each minute spent in your office as fruitful and happy as our times together outside work.

And to my team at NTC/Contemporary Books, Kara Leverte, Kim Bartko, John Nolan, Tina Chapman, and Chris Benton, who have worked with me on this our fourth book together, my gratitude for your support, hard work, and good nature.

And to all my students, who are on this journey of discovery with me, I cherish your intelligence, input, and dedication to the field of person/place.

Everything that relates, whether closely or more distantly, to psychic phenomena and to the action of psychic forces in general, should be studied just like any other science. There is nothing miraculous or supernatural in them, nothing that should engender or keep alive superstition. Psychic training, rationally and scientifically conducted, can lead to desirable results. That is why the information gained about such training—even though it is practiced empirically and based on theories to which we cannot always give assent—constitutes useful documentary evidence worthy of our attention.

—From the introduction of *Magic and Mystery in Tibet* by Alexandra David-Neel, a maverick who was the first western woman to enter the forbidden city of Lhasa in Tibet

And to you, my readers, may every day be filled with the joy of discovering and uncovering all the best in yourselves.

CONTENTS

INTRODUCTION

I f what you do at work feels like play, don't bother to read this book. But if bringing these disparate realities closer together is a goal, *Feng Shui Goes to the Office* can help. This book is designed to make work feel as satisfying as play.

I remember the last walk I took through my old neighborhood in Summit, New Jersey, before I drove away, never to return. The sloping terraces had been planted by Italian immigrants, who had flocked to this area to tend gardens on the estates of the elite. A railroad connecting this remote region with New York made Summit accessible for businesspeople who plied their trades in Manhattan's financial district.

My daily walk along this path had always been a window to the seasons' unfolding. This time the joy of viewing lilac bushes cascading over wooden slatted fences along with dogwoods and azaleas brightening this day was marred by an ache in my heart. Unlike these blossoms, I found myself in an environment that did not support my thriving. I yearned to be unfolding like spring. While work provided much in the way of comfort and conveniences, it didn't afford me the opportunity to jump into the pool of self-discovery and become my authentic self. At that moment, I decided to step aside from the known and to begin a journey, one that ultimately led me home, into my true self.

The personal journey each of us takes includes the experiences we have at work. A job ought to fill each day with joy, not just assignments to be completed. When the experience of work is aligned to one's inner being, work provides a vast forum where attitude, talent, and intelligence are expressed. Many of us expend monumental efforts trying to translate our innate gifts into marketable vehicles. Our life's progress is often measured by work's achievements; the workplace defines our worth. Character, genius, and vision are often measured by the successful interactions within the boundaries of work. Very few of us can exist without having to support survival. The form we choose becomes our profession, and its engagement becomes our calling.

The purpose of this book is to help you identify what parts of work are blissful and what parts need other supports.

To be blissful is to be in the zone, that amorphous place where time evaporates and expression joyfully consumes us. The fact that a job consumes the majority of our waking hours does not mean the workday need feel endless. The discipline of feng shui is based on the fact that an environment can alter your experiences in life. Even unpleasant tasks can be made reasonably enjoyable.

An understanding of the factors in a workplace that can add to your contentment will unfold as you comprehend feng shui's wisdom. It is my task to extricate from each of you the parts of life that you find satisfying and show you the way to incorporate them into your work life. This process can stimulate you to take quantum leaps from the status quo or aid in adjusting your work environment to support the different experiences.

By knowing which parts of a job dovetail with the highest and best parts of you, you can make any job more fulfilling. By understanding how an environment talks to you and affects experience, you can unleash untapped environmental assets that are available. Any work experience can be made more joyous by following this book's recommendations.

When J. C. Penney reached a ripe old age, he said that although his eyesight was dimming his vision had never been greater. By substantiating your intuitive vision, the ideas in this book will probably feel deeply comforting when put into practice.

Use this book as a pathfinder to self-discovery and full contentment. When work and play are equally satisfying, you have won the pot of gold waiting for you on the other side of the arched spectrum of light, the rainbow.

May you uncover your bliss.

Nancilee Wydra

PART I

THE BASICS

1

WHAT IS FENG SHUI?

*F*eng shui means "wind" and "water" in Chinese, wind being the overhead physical manifestation of the fluid mutable state of all things, water representing the fluid state of living on earth. Though this eloquently formulated discipline goes back six thousand years, the concept predates the Chinese culture. Feng shui explains how place affects the human condition, how what we see, hear, smell, and touch influences our experiences in life. The practice of examining how the physical world influences human life so as to augment the human experience goes all the way back to the earliest agrarian societies, as long ago as 8000 B.C. While hunting/gathering societies certainly had to pay attention to nature, it was agricultural societies that made an in-depth knowledge of the physical environment mandatory. To harness the physical surroundings for personal advantage required exploration of soil, sunlight, water, and topography and its influence on food production. Thus as human beings began their scramble up the ladder of knowledge, one of the first steps taken was the awareness of the place as a mandatory tool for survival.

Humans began paying attention to nature in a fresh way to determine the best conditions for growing their food. Spring floods became allies because they infused the soil with rich nutrients. Sunlight was observed to have a naturally beneficial effect on growth, while topographical conditions began to be understood in terms of their ability to advance or hinder cultivation techniques. As a body of knowledge about how the physical world influenced human life slowly grew, learning to modify the less-than-ideal factors became a natural next step. The environment became a tool not only for human survival, but also for elevating personal experience. Managing hunger birthed a sense of accomplishment and was understood to be one benefit of understanding the environment.

This is the underlying precept of the pyramid school of feng shui; an offshoot of traditional Chinese schools of feng shui. Pyramid feng shui focuses on the person and considers place a tool. Unlike traditional feng shui, pyramid feng shui suggests that we cannot create perfect feng shui until we know about the people who will occupy the space. No one person experiences his or her surroundings in exactly the same way; therefore, good feng shui can be achieved only when the individual who will occupy the place is considered. This book is based on the pyramid school of feng shui, which uses all information systems to uncover answers about why things work the way they do. I believe the pyramid school's ideas catapult feng shui into the modern world.

FORM SCHOOL

The form school, the oldest school of feng shui (still in existence since 2500 B.C.), predates any of today's civilizations. Concerned with recognizing how physical conditions influenced existence, form school practitioners were masters of observation. By studying the natural world, they could determine which side of a stream's bank would likely deteriorate and which would build up, predict the fertility of soil by locating healthy native

Form School Feng Shui

vegetation, could identify underground veins of water, could decide whether a dwelling would be cradled or stressed by the contour of a mountain, and could determine thin topsoil by the position and silhouette of stone outcroppings. During the times that human beings were initially forming stationary groups, knowledge of the best places to put down roots was essential. Agriculture gave rise to a multi-tasked community life, and culture in the arts, music, and literature began to bubble into existence.

Agriculture, of course, by allowing a society to sustain greater numbers of people, took civilization beyond that basic level of survival. With greater numbers of people living side by side, the shape of society was altered. Cities appeared, and structures became more important to life's experiences than nature. Thus, the form school's importance slowly was eroded, and the next branch of feng shui, the compass school, was born (3000 B.C.).

Compass School

When fewer and fewer people were needed to take care of more and more of the arable land, civilizations became less focused on landscape and more on human-made structures, and the compass school emerged, overshadowing the original form school.

Materialism was born when nature was no longer seen as an extension of self. A sharp decline in intimate contact with nature led to increasingly self-serving behavior. When hills were flattened or carved to support agriculture, water was transported and stored, and a network capable of transporting goods emerged, human beings lost their direct experience with natural conditions. Personal information therefore superceded natural

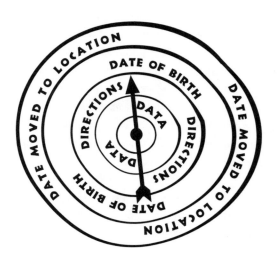

Compass Feng Shui

phenomenon and in this way, the compass school was the first feng shui system to consider the uniqueness of the individual.

The compass school originated a system to plot tangential arches around a magnetic needle. The compass school practitioner was part mathematician, part seer, and used specific formulas based on information located in up to thiry-six different rings around the center.

Living in large groups ruptures a society's intimacy as well as control. Within the framework of being known and knowing others, large groups become conceptual groups rather than contact groups. Cities are places of conceptual rather than actual intimacy. Visual symbols like flags, verbal credos like pledges and songs, and formal complex government structures are needed to enforce the group's cohesiveness and loyalty. When an individual's actions do not have immediate personal consequences, groups find it necessary to enforce written or codified rules.

BLACK SECT

After Siddhārtha Gautama (Buddha) became enlightened, his teachings were embraced by many. Ideas traveled the footpaths of itinerate preachers and trade routes. When Buddhism crossed the Himalayas, its ideas seeped into many other cultures. In Tibet, Buddhism merged with the existing religion, Bön, and the mixture became known as Tibetan Buddhism.

To understand this form of Buddhism, it is helpful to picture life on the windswept, icy steppes of the Himalayas, where flora and fauna struggled to exist. Great expanses of barren terrain made life harsh. Ideas, the only luxury, transcended the brutal existence, and it is not difficult to understand how fan-

Black Sect Feng Shui

tastic notions arose. Mystery appeared endemic, and magic seemed a reasonable remedy. Tales of teletransportation, sorcerers brewing life-sustaining elixirs, and pilgrimages lasting decades were rife. Tibetan Buddhism, a complex, exotic, extravagant cosmology, fused with form and compass feng shui when their ideas drifted over the snow capped mountain peaks (600–1200 A.D.). Today most feng shui books are written from this black sect point of view.

Like all feng shui methodologies, black sect has a symbolic language and employs remedies that embody the cultures of both the Chinese and Tibetan people. Incorporated into black sect feng shui are those customs particular to the fusion of these two cultures. However, while these customs may feel unusual, the body of knowledge examined by a black sect practitioner is similar to that investigated by other schools' practitioners. As will be discussed later in this book, connectedness, balance, and the vitality that promotes a healthy, contented life is a black sect practitioner's concern, only it may be called by other names—Tao, yin and yang, and chi.

Pyramid School Feng Shui

Pyramid school is my answer to the problem of feng shui seeming antiquated and out of date without current knowledge and cultural patterns considered. It is my belief that feng shui speaks to the issue of human experience of place. To further this field, the latest knowledge needs to be continually incorporated, for each generation, culture, or gender. Your experience of place is a unique pattern based on all the specifics of your life, from your genes to global concerns. We are a product of a vast multitude of details that ebb and flow through our lives like the wind breathing upon prairie grass. No place is experienced exactly the same way by every person. Therefore, no set of parameters can be fashioned that are absolute. In all social sciences, there is a tendency and expectation toward the general, but pyramid school practitioners honor the uniqueness of each soul and search to find the exact environmental rejoinder that supplies the impetus for change.

The pyramid school is my answer to the shortcomings of black sect feng shui for the modern world. Starting with the conclusions and suggestions that flow from ancient schools of feng shui, pyramid feng shui adds knowledge from layers of diverse disciplines with its goal of casting more and more light on the mysteries of how the physical world impacts the human experience. The pyramid school's understanding is thus continually altered by new information. As scholars probe the world to decipher the unknown, pyramid feng shui expands.

Pyramid feng shui is a singularly pragmatic science. Like all sciences, the pyramid school does not pretend to know the truth but argues that its current hypotheses take into account current facts. Pyramid feng shui seeks substantiation of its dogma from the social, physical, and esoteric sciences. When these three areas of knowledge are combined, explanations that resonate with the way we think today emerge.

As shown in the illustration on the following page, the pyramid school taps into numerous fields of study. Biology explains many human responses, while physics explains universal phenomena. Cultural and philosophical teachings are the vehicles that explain the myths and customs of a culture taught as fact to its inhabitants, thereby illuminating a belief system for the individual. From genetic proclivities to learned behavior, psychology of the individual plays a role in how experiences are ingested. Psychology investigates an individual's belief system, while sociology adds the study of cultural evolution and the effects of social systems on the individual. The individual's experience must be regarded not only in context of all of the above, but in the context of the moment. Recommendations are usually given for a period of time in an individual's experience. Like muscles that compensate when we become incapacitated by an accident or fall, once movement is experienced, it is important to re-evaluate experience in context of this change. Pyramid feng shui scrutinizes as many factors as possible within a framework of time.

Knowledge of an individual's pattern of emotional responses is sometimes the key factor in his or her experience of an environment. We all have an initial experience of place both positive and negative, and when ingredients of our primary image of place are replicated the results are individual and cannot be minimized. For example, a person who was locked in a closet may need to have a visible lock like a deadbolt or hook and eye in order to feel comfortable in a room, while a person who remembers a wallpaper pattern with affection might need a parallel complexity on wall surfaces in order to feel a place is exquisite.

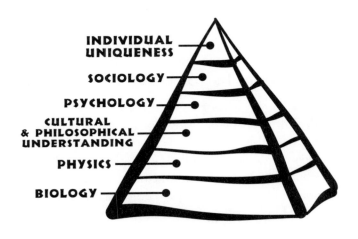

Pyramid Feng Shui

The most important revelation to emerge from the pyramid school's integration of an aggregate of knowledge is that feng shui's applications and cures (remedies for inappropriate environmental conditions) can and should be tailored specifically for each individual. Lastly, the pyramid school individualizes feng shui's cures. The pyramid school seeks to broaden the scope of feng shui cures, arguing that one icon can't possibly be the only solution to a negative condition. What is chosen to remedy a negative situation is based on personal preference and custom. For example, if a light-refracting object is sought, a cut crystal vase is as good as a geode crystal or prism glass. Wind chimes producing sound and movement as a response to air movement can be supplanted by wind socks, flags, or lightweight curtains. Suggestions in this book may be specific, but you should adjust them if they do not fit into your decor or do not reflect your beliefs or taste.

We All Live in Prison

For most of human history we lived not just in close association with nature but outdoors, in direct contact with it. Survival required full use of all of the senses. Early humans were able to identify poisonous plants by smell, discern by the sound of movement which animals lurked amid foliage, and use their vocal cords to identify themselves to others and to send signals of distress. Human beings evolved in direct response to their environment. Scientists theorize, for example, that standing upright was a response to the need to see faster predators from a safe distance.

Premodern human beings not only responded to the natural environment but also thrived in it. The sounds of birds, wind, and scurrying animals; the fragrance of grasses and flowers and the scents of animals were woven into the fabric of each day while humans performed life-sustaining tasks. The warming sunlight encouraged the production of serotonin (a neurochemical that encourages feelings of optimism and happiness) and injected vitamin D into a recipient's life force. Nature provided a multitiered sensorial infusion that is obliterated indoors.

In sharp contrast, life today in spent mostly indoors. Statistics reveal that the majority of Americans spend less than one hour outside every day. Even if we do nothing else to help our lives, spending more time outside will contribute to our physical and emotional well-being. The National Institutes of Health report that if each of us would walk twenty minutes to work and then home again at day's end, the general population's health would improve significantly.

Other ways to add time outdoors to your day are simple: Start the day by stepping outside and take ten deep breaths just outside the front door. Eschew home newspaper delivery and walk to buy a morning paper. Sweep the path to your home or front steps. Walk around the perimeter of your home. Walk around the block.

In addition to getting outside, you can make your indoor space more representative of the natural world. A basic goal of pyramid feng shui is to replicate all sensorial experiences indoors. It is important to do this not just because the outdoor environment is life-giving, but also because living indoors is essentially living in prison. Hunters and gatherers of the past moved indoors when the plow eliminated the need for everyone to be outside farming, but the seeking of shelter goes back much further. Interior spaces were probably first used to conceal valuable resources from theft, store food, and protect life and limb from animals or marauders. In other words, human beings originally separated themselves from nature out of fear, seeking safety from environmental threats. We protect ourselves from adverse elements in our environment today as well. Although the end result of safety and security is positive, the motivation is not. It is far better to be motivated by joy and ecstasy than by fear and uncertainty.

In the dark reaches of our collective psyche there is the knowledge that by sequestering ourselves indoors we acknowledge that we are captives of fear. We have structured our societies to prevent fear far more frequently than to motivate self-actualization, and this is why feng shui cures are so often needed. Any replication of natural surroundings can be an antidote to dread.

Knowledge of feng shui helps us fulfill our deepest desire, which is to live unfettered by fear. To be in optimum health, expressing who we are powerfully and articulately, to be in community with others, and to engage our best and highest talents are the basic elements of contentment. Toward that end, this book unveils ways you can alter your work environment to create conditions that your biology and spirit crave. The aim is to be free from fear, to feel affirmed, and to know that you have a support system on which to rely. When the environment meets these core human needs, our work spaces become a foundation for personal fulfillment.

2

WHAT IS WORK?

W hen my son Zachary was young, he used to play a game called "days of the living." It consisted of surviving an entire day by his own ingenuity. All things eaten, used, or accomplished had to be a direct result of personal effort. I know it was cheating to fill his father's canteen with water when I sent him off to roam the nearby woods with our loyal golden retriever, Oakie. Before setting off into the unknown, Zac would pilfer vegetables from the garden, which he helped plant each year, stuffing his jeans pockets with carrots that he would wash in the waters of the creek. When he returned, he would regale me with stories of how he'd constructed a tepee of fallen branches to rest under or how Oakie had enthusiastically retrieved mountains of pinecones tossed in the air. Then Zac would unload his treasures—paraphernalia left in the woods by seasonal hunters, collections of stones, and occasionally a toad. Duplicating the activities of our forebears, Zachary was engaged in what hunter-gatherers considered merely life. We call it work.

Survival was our ancestors' work objective. No one was hired or fired from a job, because anyone who could not perform one task was either reassigned or had died. Very few lived without contributing to survival efforts. We have many more choices. One of the aims of this book is to help you find work that is so intrinsic to your nature that you will love it.

Back when humans roamed the earth hunting and gathering, it took three or four hours of labor to supply life's necessities for each day. The rest of the day was reserved for socializing and other personally satisfying activities. Our ancestors had ample time to muse, visit, chat, and savor life. For most of us, three or four hours of leisure each day would be considered an enormous treat. Today, work so dominates our lives that even play is described with work verbiage. We work out to tone our bodies, complete homework when taking courses to improve our minds, work on committees and charities, and tell our family that dinner is in the works. We expect life to be an exercise of exertion.

When early-nineteenth-century futurists imagined a brave new world, they didn't envision workers spending more time at work than at home. Modern life was supposed to provide equal time to enjoy leisure activities. A host of factors contributed to the extension of the workday and diminishment of leisure, increasing this disparity of time. Life, it was perceived, was blighted by a workplace where concern about products and results far outstripped concern for the human experience.

Today direct remedies have been implemented to counteract centuries of worker abuse. Civility, equality, and safety are now infused into labor laws that companies are bound to obey. Yet, while today's workplace might be safer, it is not necessarily more gratifying.

Job satisfaction depends on a hierarchy of needs that can be met not only by legislation and human services but also by the physical environment. Successful industries have learned to discern what feedback their physical plant provides. The widgets or services flow effortlessly from their doors when all parts of the whole are in order. Unfortunately, the physical environment is often overlooked altogether when emotional satisfaction of employees is being addressed. Companies spend huge sums on architectural and design services to make a workplace aesthetically pleasing as well as safe and efficient, yet still these spaces may not improve overall company performance or job satisfaction.

Most of us have gone on at least one job interview where our immediate reaction to the workplace was "Oh, my goodness, I'd never want to work here!" But can you articulate what in the environment contributed to this negative feeling? Uncovering factors that contribute to a quality of unfriendliness, emotional bleakness, or uncomfortable isolation is one benefit of learning feng shui. When we can identify what is not beneficial in an environment, we can avoid making the choices that bring about discomfort.

When I was growing up, my father arrived home each day promptly at 6:00 P.M. How many of you end your day at the proverbial 5:00 or even at a predictable time? Probably not too many. If we are unable to change the amount of time we spend at work, then we should at least seek work that fits us in a more supportive way. We should insist on infusing a job with those qualities that nurture. We should work in surroundings we love, which support the realization of our goals.

Communication between a person and the place he or she inhabits is key to blazing a blissful life path. Your job can be a joy when you understand how to set up a work experience to benefit your particular personality.

Despite tremendous social shifts and fond notions of progress, the foundations of human needs haven't changed much. What have changed are the requisites. Perhaps we have been programmed to crave material possessions more than experiences.

Are the material rewards camouflaging the emotional and spiritual impact of the encounter? If we could stand back and see the way stretching before us, we would see that we have been forced to separate life into two paths, the path of high technology and the path of high sensation.

High Technology Versus High Sensation

As populations grew and towns and cities came into existence, diversification overtook the simple life in which everyone provided for his or her own survival needs. More intangible needs springing from the world of ideas now had to be satisfied along with basic survival needs. Tasks that did not have a direct bearing on survival could now be exchanged for food and shelter. Thus the concept of work as we know it today was born.

Also born at this time was the high-tech path in life, the path on which acquisition of things supersedes emotional benefits. The high-tech path objectifies goals and holds quantifiable production in high esteem. Once no one person, family, or even neighborhood supplied the composite goods for its own needs, the emotional satisfaction of surviving by one's wits and of seeing the product of one's labor was denied to many. When individuals cannot substantially recognize their contribution to the whole, emphasis is shifted from pride in accomplishments and satisfaction in the process to efficiency, speed, and the value of exchange. When we work for symbolic rewards or money rather than tangible experiences, we lose the joy of working at that which gives us the greatest pleasure, completion or engagement in a whole process.

In contrast to the high-technology path, the high-sensation path celebrates internal experiences and values positive emotional connections. A building could take decades to erect, but if there is pride in replicating a design handed down through generations, there is joy in the work. When we know what our personal contributions to the work are, we are connected directly with the product. Paths of high sensation offer the continuity of full participation in the process and a sense of enmeshment with the past combined with respect for the future. Although the high-sensation path has not been completely obliterated from the workplace, it certainly has been relegated to the backseat.

CURING THE HIGH-TECHNOLOGY WORKPLACE

Work situations that are high-tech rather than high-sensation produce negative symptoms. High-tech surroundings often exude feelings of strain and tension, isolation, and obsession. Strain and tension cause irritability, make us feel isolated from others, and feed our tendency to obsess over work content.

Removing physical manifestations that give rise to physical, mental, and spiritual ill health is the goal of office feng shui. Feng shui can correct workplace imbalances by creating conditions that we were biologically predestined to experience and by altering factors in the environment that elicit negative emotional responses.

If you are experiencing strain, tension, isolation, or needless obsession, see if the causative conditions described in the following sections exist. If they do, consider implementing the cures listed.

Strain and Tension

Strain is a feeling of being held back or pulled in one direction, while tension implies being stretched in both directions and not being able to satisfy any demands. Both are contemporary diseases causing illness, feelings of impotency, and the belief that life is a struggle. Underlying feng shui is the notion that while gloom and stagnation are not easy to alter, changes made in a physical environment can lessen them. After selecting the definition of strain or tension that fits your situation, review the choices for how to alter your workplace to lighten any strain or tension.

Strain

Do you feel annoyed if someone interrupts you while working? Do you have trouble remembering where you placed a file or a piece of paper? If you find yourself getting exasperated frequently during the course of a day, you may be suffering from the kind of strain that certain conditions intensify. Strain separates us from ourselves as well as our interactions with others. It causes us to feel fettered beyond comfortable limits and thwarted in general. In very small doses strain can stimulate growth, but when ongoing it causes us to become unglued. When under strain, we tend to construct walls in our psyche that no rational mental processes can penetrate. Strain makes us edgy and quick tempered and leaves us feeling exhausted, unfulfilled, and frustrated. Strain makes us seek a perpetrator and exhibit displaced anger toward a human target or targets. Ultimately, strain may cause us to be confrontational and feel friction with or isolation from co-workers.

The worst consequence of strain is its potential to erode satisfying human contact. When under strain any organism seeks to withdraw and heal. In some ways it is like having an open wound that cannot be touched and is eased only by screening or detachment from outside contact. Living with ongoing strain destroys morale, health, and the enjoyment of satisfying relationships. Naturally, it is best to reverse the physical conditions that give rise to strain.

Strain can be caused by an abundance of reflective surfaces. File cabinets, steel desks, and a plethora of office equipment made of highly polished plastic and wood surfaces flood work environments with reflective surfaces that draw the eye and pull us away from work on our desktops. Like a peephole in a solid wall, the shiny surface attracts our eye more than other surfaces. It also forces us to think, creating a continuous loop between our perception of the object and our interpretation of it. Shiny metal exaggerates the mental process, and the typical office literally forces us to vibrate with cerebral activities. No wonder we feel strained.

In the same way as we are drawn to stare into a candle's flickering flame not only because it emanates light but also because it moves. Moving, reflective surfaces are particularly hypnotic. Therefore, in many work spaces computer screens compete for our attention. Mesmerizing, stimulating surfaces, like thorns piercing the skin, should be removed or minimized. Although metallic file cabinets and other highly polished surfaces don't physically move, the continuous reflection of light from them forces us to look at them repeatedly, as if a moving object was continually coming into our peripheral vision.

Try covering a desktop or a file cabinet with a nonshiny fabric such as black felt. Black, a color related to the water element, is calming and emotionally centering. Covering a desktop with a matte black surface will reduce strain.

Sharing office space with large numbers of people also causes strain. Feeling cocooned and separate is, according to eminent cultural anthropologist Edward T. Hall, distinctly Western. Westerners need more physical space surrounding

How much space do you need to feel comfortable and unencumbered?

them than people of other cultures. In an office, space of at least five feet beyond our bodies' boundaries is our requirement for feeling comfortable. Insufficient space makes us sequester ourselves from others, mentally and emotionally.

Tension

Tension causes us to feel pulled by at least two things at once beyond a range we find comfortable. Tension can be caused by repetitive acts or actions that exceed our capacity to tolerate. Imagine, for example, hating heights and having to walk across a ledge several times a day instead of once in a blue moon. Continually being tested by challenging situations leads to a state of tension. Tension builds up anxiety, suspense, and an intensity that is wearing on the psyche. Over time, tension can deplete our will to accommodate others, forcing us to give up trying, or run away from successfully completing tasks.

Work spaces with a high level of tension may experience high turnover.

Lighting Influences Mood Humans are biologically designed to live outside. Sunlight contains all colors of the spectrum and triggers production of serotonin, a neurochemical that can make us feel euphoric and optimistic. We tend to be empathetic and careful in our communications when we feel good but abrupt and charged when tense. In contrast, unlike the fluorescent lights so common in offices, full spectrum lights illuminate the surroundings with an array of colors that help induce good feelings.

Perhaps you're familiar with the syndrome SAD (seasonal affective disorder), a type of depression caused by lack of exposure to sunlight. When not surrounded by light with a full complement of colors, we are denied a natural opiate. Replicating natural lighting indoors can reduce depression and general malaise at work. Moreover, cones of light created by spotlights, tabletop lamps, wall sconces, and floor lamps produce a more natural atmosphere than a room lit by overhead fixtures and will light a space in a pattern closer to sunlight's dappled rays.

If you cannot control the entire atmosphere in your workplace, place a lamp with a full-spectrum lightbulb on your desk. If the cone of light encircles your body, tension is more likely to melt away, like an ice cube on a hot summer day.

Ambient Sound Versus Ambient Noise Have you ever noticed how a particular noise dominates an environment only after it disappears? Ongoing mechanical noises—the hum of a computer, the screeching of a fax machine, and the buzz of fluorescent lights, all typical of most offices—can wear you down. While we do not register them consciously, they are still experienced negatively, largely because they seem almost fused into a setting.

If you think about it, you'll realize that what is experienced as pleasant natural sounds are almost never constant. Even the babbling of a brook or the splashing of waves surrounds us with subtle auditory variety, while mechanical sounds do not. In most natural settings an ongoing flurry of sounds emanates from all sorts of sources, treading lightly on our senses but still stimulating them with little surprises.

Mentally step outside as if you are leaving your home for work. Perhaps the first sound you hear is of the door closing behind you. The slap of your shoe on the pavement and the crunch it makes on stones barely register because you are listening to a squirrel scurry across the ground while, in the distance, a bird chirps. Within a short time the rumbling of an automobile becomes distinct, and far away a horn toots. These auditory melodies continue until you reach your destination. Once inside, however, you are surrounded by a predictable nonstop hum of sounds that vary little during the forty or more hours you spend weekly in this environment. This exceeds your capacity for auditory sameness and creates tension.

To correct the problem, don't simply try to obliterate those sounds. Silence is no more natural than monotony, so it is good feng shui to introduce a variety of sounds. It is not difficult to replace ambient noise with ambient sound in an office. You already benefit from some variety in the form of footsteps crossing a variety of flooring, sometimes teakettles whistling, coffee makers slurping, and cabinet drawers being opened and shut. Often just by walking through an office you can hear different radio stations or fingers tap-dancing their way over a computer's keyboard in different rhythms. All these sounds are woven into an association with a place of business. A clock with birds chirping on the hour, a Winchester clock with four different songs tolling on the quarter hour, a cuckoo clock, or unlike bells looped over door handles can add to variety throughout the day. If you have more than one clock making sounds, set one timepiece ahead or behind the hour so that each one chimes independently. Perhaps those sharing an office should program different sounds on their computers, filling each office with unique melodies.

This variety becomes the voice of the space, with a unique character that, if you stop and listen, is instantly familiar. Any space in which we spend a great deal of time must satisfy us on all sensorial levels, and sound is, unfortunately, one that is often ignored. Are the melodies in your workplace favorable? Do they soothe, delight, and add a rhythm to each day? If not, here is a list of pleasant sounds that can be added to any workplace.

Sound Devices to Consider Adding to an Office

Chirping clock
Cuckoo clock
Winchester clock
Bells attached to doors
Varied flooring
Whistling teakettles
Programmed computer sounds and voices
Wind chimes near air vents
Open windows to permit window treatments to flap

Isolation

Human beings clearly are not meant to live isolated and alone. We are helpless for a longer period of time than other species, and modern culture prolongs the maturation process even further. Modern life complicates matters even more. We have become accustomed to a chain of dependency on others that, while not appearing fragile, has the capacity to be devastating. The oil crisis of the 1970s shook us up because it was the first time since World War II when freedom of movement was snatched from the individual's control. Even when we want to stay at arm's length from others, we are enmeshed in a deeply complicated chain that has links far from our personal reach.

Today's workplace is similarly fragile. The sense of companionship and intimacy may be wiped out by the stroke of a pen. Receiving a termination notice banishes the individual not only from a livelihood but also from a network of individuals with whom she or he has developed intimacy. Underscoring all workplace associations is the underlying knowledge that we can be or choose to be exiled at any time. Perhaps this causes many to construct an invisible shield against emotional vulnerability and to avoid deep intimate relationships.

We have, in fact, halved and in some cases quartered our links of intimacy in favor of autonomy and career advancement. While relocating can be a heartfelt choice, more often than not career choices are the impetus for changing cities, states, or countries. In making these moves we continue a march toward individual isolation fueled by mobility that has already scattered us to places where we are unknown. What we give up for mobility is our network of intimacies, and it is not uncommon for us to spend our final years surrounded by people with whom we have had no previous contact.

Being connected is so fundamental to a fulfilling existence that our very contentment often depends on restructuring the places of business where we spend much of each day. Creating a context for being an appropriate part of an interdependent whole and embracing the need for interconnectedness are the challenges of today's workplace.

Isolation Can Be Caused by Absence of Scents

We are not nearly aware of how important scent is to a full and healthy life. Adjectives describing sight, sound, and touch are easier to access than ones conveying the experience of scent. Consider the shape, color, and scent of a rose. Words flow forth easily when describing the velvety petals glowing with a warm, heart-stopping red. However, coming up with words describing the scent of a rose is much more difficult. Ironically, when the first land life forms crawled out of the primordial soup, their sense of smell was their only way to comprehend an environment. They did not see or hear. So important was the olfactory sensor that it sat atop the brain stem. Evolution may have given us new ways of experiencing our world, but the sense of smell remains a primary connection to life. Without scents we are isolated from the basic experience of life.

Scent can increase loquaciousness. Before a lecture, I often have an assistant stand at the entrance and offer attendees a choice of fragrances to smell. Then I watch as complete strangers begin conversing as they wait for the presentation to begin. Introducing fragrance can enhance conversation and foster lively interaction. Scent preceding a brainstorming session can be effective or, for purposes of connection, scent can increase camaraderie.

Even when no fragrance is intentionally added to an office, a variety of scents from people, office machinery, air, and food floats through the air, giving each workplace its own distinct sensorial brew. What is lacking in most indoor spaces is an assortment of scents comprising diverse categories. A scent-deprived environment must be filled with a variety of scents, not just one. Just as the natural world is filled with a variety of sounds, in nature there is an intermingling of many fragrances. This mixture increases or decreases in intensity and changes character depending on location, the movement of our currents, and the temperature.

Since each category of scent evokes specific emotions, it is wise to consider what kind of feelings of enmeshment and belonging would be best in your workplace.

CATEGORIES OF SCENT	EXAMPLES OF SCENTS	RESPONSES EVOKED
Floral	rose, gardenia, jasmine, lavender	intimacy
Ethereal	pear, banana, grapefruit	inspiration to connect
Acrid	metals, vinegar	discrimination
Minty	pine, cedar, peppermint	energy and involvement
Musky	musk	arousal and stimulation

Obsession

When you spend your leisure time thinking about work obligations, you have begun to obsess. Obsessions can be an extreme preoccupation or a phantom delusion focused on pieces of reality. Either way, when you devote a great deal of thought to one aspect of work or one task, the other parts of the whole will suffer, and so will you. When the host of a dinner party becomes overfocused on having enough desserts, he or she dilutes the potential to have a good time. A parent of a disabled child may give so much attention to that child that the other siblings wilt from lack of attention. An overabundant sense of commitment to life's tasks may seem admirable from the outside, but invariably it will cause other areas of life to atrophy. Obsessing limits options and like a whirlpool sucks variety from life.

Clutter Can Contribute to Obsessing and Workaholic Behavior

Remember thinking computers would create a paperless office? Have you stopped laughing yet? If you have ever had a computer crash or lose important content, you might now be a compulsive printer of all documents.

A few days before the deadline for my last book, *Look Before You Love: Feng Shui Techniques for Revealing Anyone's True Nature*, I placed my coffee mug on a pile of paper that tilted dangerously toward my computer. To my horror, as I released the cup's handle I watched the shiny blue National Public Radio mug slide off the pile onto my laptop. With a pop and a sizzle, my entire book disappeared. The story had a happy ending, for the brain was retrieved and the backup tape worked, and I was able to submit the book a mere one week late. However, the emotional residue was frightening. To quell my growing fear of a computer crash, I printed every single document I wrote. The need to tame the paper tiger became critical.

Replacing an L-shaped desk with a simple three- by six-foot rectangular one, I was forced to reduce what had been amassed on top of my desk. Refining, reducing, clearing, and throwing away seemed to alter the structure of my workplace, and this principle can work for you too. Instead of adding more storage, remove a surface, a cabinet, or a file from a work space and see how unhealthy preoccupations retract.

I don't have to tell you that paper clutter reduces work quality as well as personal comfort. Elementary as it may appear, the first task is to pick up all work items from the floor. Then organize like things together, such as all books, office supplies, files, etc., and evaluate which demand to be close by and which can be stored out of view.

Inspiration to Help You Organize Office Clutter Select a time of the day when you are typically not as productive as normal. This will alleviate guilt about not "working." For a reasonably short period of time, such as ten to twelve minutes (it's useful to use an actual timer or set an alarm clock), select the oldest pile of clutter in your office, and separate it into three piles: "File" pile, "Throw Away" pile, or "I Still Might Do This" pile. Hopefully, the oldest pile will have out-of-date activities that you can throw away. Remember, you are not to work longer than the preset time. Time framing allows you to feel a sense of accomplishment without forcing you to do the entire task.

Order and prioritizing eliminate obsessing, but if these steps don't visually unclutter your office, you can enhance your ability to focus by placing a clear crystal paperweight or any colorless object that refracts light near the mess to divert attention away. Being attracted to an object that refracts light can loosen the grip of obsession.

CREATING A HIGH-SENSATION WORKPLACE

The path of high sensation proposes that you look within and realign your interior experiences with your day-to-day living. The fascinating aspect of living fully aware is that it requires a hands-off approach.

Living in the Flow

You may have noticed that the more you try, the less consistent are the results. This frequently happens with my tennis game. Since my work involves a great deal of travel, I often miss one or more weekly games, and I used to fear that these interruptions would send my game into a tailspin. Was I wrong! Imagine my surprise when I returned home and discovered that my game had actually improved.

This phenomenon has been studied extensively. One research project compared the basketball skills of one group, which was given daily on-court foul shot training, with those of another, which was closeted in a classroom and asked to visualize improving their free throws. After two weeks, the results were identical; both groups had enhanced their performances equally. Contemplation, it appears, can be as profound as actual practice, a principle I must have benefited from unwittingly by visualizing myself making perfect ground strokes while out of town.

To be in the flow can be experienced by simply being. To allow events to take their course should feel the same as allowing one's own pulse to beat in its personal time. Once you have gotten into your flow, improvements follow naturally. The posture of the wise is one of witnessing. When we detach ourselves from the emotional fray, all things can be considered.

Like many in the generation of the 1960s, I had developed a confrontational approach to life. When I viewed injustice, I voiced my dissatisfaction loudly. When I felt a wrong, I marched headfirst into the mayhem until anyone I perceived as my opponent was battered and exhausted. I seemed always to be embroiled in conflict—until the day I was gassed in an industrial accident.

My wrath at the corporation whose lax safety precautions permitted this violation made me hunger to rectify this industrial hazard. However, before I could begin this process, my scarred lungs needed to heal, and I retreated to a well-known holistic center run by a well-respected guru. I was stunned by the response I got when I sought his guidance as to whether I should intervene legally in the company's operation to force it to alter a dangerous procedure.

Do nothing, I was advised. Expressing rage would only focus the company on reacting to my wrath. Without it they would have to deal with the truth. I followed his advice and guess what they did? Within four months the department whose toxins were diffused into the workplace was closed down.

Sometimes all we need to do is get out of our own way for the light to shine.

Living in the flow precludes not forcing resolution of each and every issue. It can be as simple as listening to approaching footsteps or closing your eyes when speaking over the telephone to snuff out distractions and be fully present. Like warming your hands in the heat emanating from a lightbulb, taking time for things to unfold fosters high sensation.

Belonging

Feeling enmeshed in and part of a process advances our sense of belonging. *Belonging* means being integrated in the whole with an awareness and respect for each part. Belonging vests us with responsibility for the well-being of the process, not just ourselves. With this caring we gain the stamina to pursue excellence and protect that which sustains us far more forcefully than any material possession ever could.

Belonging can be articulated in feng shui terms in the following ways:

- Having the right to decorate the space surrounding your work area

- Having a niche for personal belongings outside the immediate work space
- Having a favorite blend of tea, coffee, or water available
- Having a nameplate on your desk or workbench
- Feeling as if your input is valued and considered when changes or alterations are contemplated

Focus

Peak performance requires efficient use of time. Dithering away hours gathering your thoughts or tools for work is exhausting and lets the best creative juices leak. Have you ever eaten at your desk? When doing so, both eating and what you are trying to accomplish suffer. Interrupting thoughts to take a bite out of a sandwich or turning away from a conversation to sip from a mug can disrupt the smooth transition between thought and form (performance). If you are not accomplishing what you plan, concentrate on only one process at a time. Changes in your environment can help too:

- Keep movement from passageways out of range of your peripheral vision. Based on our survival responses, random movement attracts the eye.
- Face toward the entrance door of a room. We relax fully when facing an area of penetration.
- Remove clutter from the top of a desk. A great deal of unfinished work in view is anxiety provoking, and anxiety dissipates concentration.
- Eat when hungry. Hunger hinders sharp concentration.
- Savor a peppermint. It signals satiation to the brain.

- Rub a few drops of clary sage essential oil on the tip of your nose. Clary sage dissipates feelings of restlessness.
- Position a small desktop fan to keep a light current of air circulating around your desk area. Motionless air enervates, while slight movement energizes.
- Place a black desk pad under your keyboard or writing surface. Because black gives the illusion of depth, it is one way to add dimensional variety to avoid feeling restrained.

To love what we do, it is important to gift ourselves with supports to stimulate freshness, aliveness, and enmeshment. After all, to work is a way of being, and to be is to encounter all that we as a species are meant to experience—light, air, depth, scent, sound, safety, belonging, support, joy, and finally self-actualization. Therefore, when work embraces what is essential for contentment, life becomes an effortless endeavor, rising from the soul as an ocean's spray meeting the air.

3

WHAT DO I NEED?

D o not resign yourself to having little control over the physical working environment. Just as being warm, fed, and cuddled is central to an infant's maturation, the spaces we work in are the fulcrum for effective performance. Search your soul to determine if your basic needs are being met. If not, make changes.

Abraham Maslow, the noted psychologist, pointed out that people feel fulfilled only when a hierarchy of needs is met. Physical survival is the basic need. After that, feeling secure and safe is essential to effective functioning. We absorb the world around us through all our senses. Therefore, many messages are transferred to our experience on the subconscious level. In fact, when asked why one office or one workstation is better than another, it takes time to discern and finally articulate why.

The following is Maslow's list of needs and an interpretation of how they may be expressed in a work environment. Score from one to five points with one being the lowest and five the highest. For example, if your desk is placed under an overhead light and a desk lamp is also provided, you might give task lighting a score of five. Conversely, if your desk is midway between two overhead lights casting shadows in the center of your workstation, you might want to score one for task lighting. Answer all questions subjectively. Do not try to analyze or make excuses.

Need	Environmental Condition	Score
Physiological	Temperature comfort	
	Adequate task lighting	
	Noise level	
	Smells or odors	
Safety	Outside building	
	On stairs or elevator	
	Seeing door to your work area	
	In rest room	
Belonging	Workstation position	
	Conference or meeting area seating position (feel as if you are close to decision maker)	
	Specialized people role in office (distribute checks, purchase break supplies, order lunch, etc.)	
	Association with others outside of business hours	
	Visual representations of your contribution (ideas suggested that have been implemented, awards, etc.)	
Self-Esteem	Ability to personalize your work area	
	Direct access to authority figures	
	Reasonable rules to follow	
Self-Actualization	Opportunities for learning (library, allowance to buy books, take classes, etc.)	
	Empowerment to question procedures and access to decision maker	
	Challenge to advance	
	Clearly set goals and rewards	
Self-Transcendence	Experience the all in each segment of the process	
	Truly relish anyone's positive experiences	
	Understand the network of support and are unencumbered by it	
	Can experience the I in all persons, places, or things	

Let's look at how each area relates to different feng shui categories. You will be surprised to see that adjusting conditions slightly can exponentially speed your progress toward contentment while eliminating unconstructive situations.

PHYSIOLOGICAL AND SENSORIAL EXPERIENCES

Physiological needs relate to direct sensorial experiences. Is the office warm or cool enough? Is the scent of the office varied and acceptable to you? Do you have to strain to see clearly or fight insidious noise to concentrate on the task at hand? When physical needs are not met, the ability to work may be undermined. Just as it is helpful to organize your desk at the start of each day, an acceptable physical space is central to effective productivity and contentment.

Consider a person standing outside on a subzero day waiting for a bus. Feeling physically punished, the person's entire focus is likely to be on how long the wait will be before the bus arrives. All other thoughts quickly slide into oblivion in the face of physical discomfort.

Mental and social focus cannot begin until physical needs are met. If you have ever shouted out loud inappropriately when you stubbed your toe or used an expletive when a sharp object pierced your skin, you know social decorum is not the first concern when provoked physically. Employers who are ignoring sensory experiences are asking their employees to expend superhuman efforts to work at their highest and most effective level. In a free society, such demands will not be tolerated for long.

SAFETY AND LOCATION

Safety is fundamental to our capacity to thrive, yet often it is not consciously taken into account when planning, developing, and configuring space.

In the workplace a great deal of attention is paid instead to the safety of information. The risk of losing productivity or revenues and liability exposure drive owners to ensure that premises are accident-proof, but the safety referred to by Maslow reaches more deeply into the human psyche. Fear never crosses your mind when you profoundly believe that you are being kept out of harm's way. The miracle of safety is produced when those responsible for creating your work space make you unaware of danger.

Generally we feel safe only when we have control of or access to the contained areas in which we must work. The amount of control we require depends on culture, location, and recent history. If your workplace is in an area that is perceived as unsafe, you will feel less anxious riding the elevator when the only way someone can use it is to sign in at a security station. When a stairwell or parking garage is busy, rest rooms are within the confines of the office, or there is a doorman or guard by the entrance gate, you are more likely to feel safe than in the absence of these conditions.

In areas outside of cities, perception of safety is subtler. Access to help may be the necessary ingredient. Finding yourself in a car that won't start, slipping on a slick surface, or alone in a building might evoke feelings of danger.

Determine what constitutes safety for your area. It's that moment of hesitation that surrounds an experience or the fear of an experience that defines personal security.

BELONGING AND PROXIMITY

Have you ever experienced a group hug? If you have, you know it feels better to be in the center than at the perimeter. Being in the thick of things, being central in an organization, creates a sensation of belonging and a connection that binds you to work in an important way. Feeling part of, or belonging to, is likely to contribute to a desire to care about producing results. Proximity is the first physical manifestation of belonging.

In traditional feng shui there is an adage that workers assigned a desk closest to an exit door are viewed as most dispensable. The placement of a workstation is the physical representation of your worth.

An office functions best when laid out with a center. A comparison between the way cities are laid out in European capitals and our American cities may best illustrate what happens when a heart or center is not fixed in an office design.

Does your workplace have discernible hearts? When every road converges in one plaza or another, you feel as if you are always arriving at the heart of an area, no matter where you are in a city. Each plaza is a heart, and in a large corporation this could be represented by each department. Yet no heart or department is separated from easy and identifiable access to other hearts or departments. You are in the center when inside each plaza's perimeter. When all roads lead to Rome, you wander with confidence.

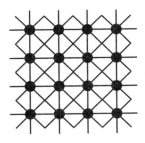

Cities designed with plazas, as in Europe, have all roads leading to centers or hearts.

Unlike Old World cities laid out with plazas defining space, the configuration of most American cities is linear. Roads follow straight lines without benefit of a distinctive public marker along the way. Do the pathways in your office lead nowhere?

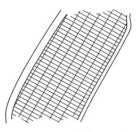

Dissecting straight roads, typical in the United States, lead nowhere.

SELF-ESTEEM AND PERSONAL EXPRESSION

My friends Rick and Joanne have a one-year-old who has yet to learn to speak. When he is unable to communicate his needs, his frustration level mounts quickly and acutely. Anyone who has reared a child or cared for an animal knows that when needs can't be interpreted, discomfort and rage escalate.

Back to our person at the bus stop. He decides to throw frugality to the wind and makes a cell phone call home even though the call will be outrageously expensive. Being able to share his miserable experience with a loved one helps soothe his soul and helps time evaporate. Likewise, many of us have experienced the reversal of negative feelings when given permission to voice discomfort. When someone is there to listen to your concerns, distress can roll away as naturally as water flows down a hill. When we feel listened to, our self-esteem skyrockets and the nagging sense of being out of the loop, out of control, or out of luck can be assuaged.

Being listened to is beneficial not only in challenging situations but also when conditions are favorable. How many people do you know who want to write a book? They have a story, a computer, and some reasonable time to write but still are unable to begin. I suspect the number of would-be authors exceeds the number of actual ones by a huge margin. What separates those who fulfill their desires from those who don't? Self-esteem.

Personal expression implies a forum in which one is understood, nurtured, and appreciated. Self-esteem requires being accepted and respected. I suspect that those who don't live their dreams don't believe in themselves and are surrounded by others who don't believe in them either. Therefore, what separates those who do from those who don't is a place in which personal expression is acknowledged and nourished.

The seeds of self-esteem are planted firmly in the soil of heart-felt acknowledgments.

SELF-ACTUALIZATION AND AUTONOMOUS DEVELOPMENT

When the person at the bus stop hangs up the phone, a plan pops into his mind. "What if I call a cab? Sure it's much more expensive, but I deserve this luxury." With that he pulls out his cell phone again and dials salvation. Warmed by the prospect of being whisked back home momentarily, he notices the bus lumbering along in the distance. Punching the redial button on his phone, he barks at the radio dispatcher to cancel his cab. In a few short seconds he has taken control of his life and made self-serving decisions that give him a feeling of empowerment and satisfaction.

To feel content, we must take control of life's situations and seize opportunities that acknowledge the hierarchy of needs. Actualization requires taking charge of life events to restore or infuse personal balance in all situations. The business of life includes the self-needs fundamental to this process. Physical comfort, safety, belonging, self-esteem, and opportunities for self-actualization are fundamental in any hierarchy to encourage the highest functioning.

The interesting thing about this ladder of needs is that we cannot start at the top. Similar to the stages of infant development, we need to secure the most basic before we can focus on more advanced needs. A baby who cannot sit certainly can't crawl, and one who doesn't vocalize sounds will have a difficult time learning to form words. In fact child psychologists tell us that an infant who skips a stage on the developmental ladder will have a harder time with subsequent maturation. The child who doesn't crawl at the appropriate stage may grow into the adult who isn't capable of following instructions easily.

Humans stand alone in having a complex system of storing and retrieving information in the part of the brain called the *neocortex*. This part of the brain can intercede, extrapolate, insert, and interpret information in ways other life forms cannot. This innate ability gives humans the capacity to perceive interactions differently from other creatures and broadens the scope of self exponentially.

If a bubble were drawn around each one of us, the bubble would include a specific physical location—the neighborhood and workplace—as well as friends and relatives wherever they are. Each one of us has a gigantic bubble that includes and enfolds our known world. And like the difference between a simple eight-piece jigsaw puzzle for a two-year-old and one that has hundreds of pieces, the human condition is far more complex than the world of other living things.

What is so interesting about self-actualization is that it is not strictly an internal process. What is "out there" affects what is "in here." That is, you will be able to actualize your talents only to the extent that you can interpret and harness signals from the environment. What emerges from this understanding is that your environment is instrumental to your development, right down, it seems, to your DNA.

According to cell biologist Bruce Lipton, Darwinian theory is not scientific "truth." He had no real scientific proof for his theory of survival of the fittest. Darwinian theory, with its emphasis on random mutations as a source of evolution is a strictly metaphysical concept. It is not scientifically possible to test a theory that is based upon "random" events or chance. Darwin's theory that new traits are passed down from one generation to another originally by chance is incorrect. Randomness and chaos fly in the face of everything we have learned about the way the universe works. If randomness existed, how would scientists at NASA be able to calculate the precise energy needed for a rocket to reach the moon? We live in a world built sequentially in an order that, while not entirely known, can be counted on to be predictable.

Fifty years before Darwin's time, a theory of evolution was proposed by the Frenchman Jean-Baptiste Lamarck, stating that those who are most able to adapt to their environment are the best candidates for survival. He theorized that evolution is a result of an organism's organization in response to its environment. For instance, a blacksmith's arms will become muscular as a result of his trade, and his children will have this "strong arm" potential passed down to them. Lamarck said that it is the environment that drives a species' progression and change.

Fascinated by Lamarck's theory, Lipton set out to uncover how this might be true on a cellular level. The results of his research gave Lipton an explanation for the veracity of Lamarck's theory. In an experiment, genetically identical seeds were planted in distinctly different environments. The seeds had been taken from one single plant and therefore had the same DNA. They were then placed in planters with different soils, moisture, sunlight, and locations. In other words, each location required different constitutions for survival. When each seed matured into a plant, its seeds were examined to determine if the DNA had remained identical. The results revealed that at maturation the DNA of each plant's seed was altered. The parent plant had produced genetically different progeny. Each plant had adapted uniquely to its environment and passed this adaptation via altered DNA to its progeny.

Lipton extrapolates that environmental conditions initiated change. The plants had been able to read accurately the dis-

According to Lamarck, mutated genes are not random occurrences.
We pass on to our offspring those traits that developed in
response to our environment.

tinct environmental needs and been able to procure selectively
from their own genetic potential traits that served survival best
in that particular location. To understand this concept it is helpful to picture DNA as a series of different software programs.
Just like the software programs in your computer, they are not
used until you open them. When you want to work on finances,
you open the supporting software; when you want to log on
to the Internet, you open your Web server, etc.

What is so interesting about his theory is that scientists discovered in this century that we have DNA we don't use. They
called this *junk DNA*. Lipton extrapolates that this supposed junk
is similar to software waiting to be called up for service. The
blacksmith whose muscles developed prodigiously had within
his DNA that potential, which was activated by environmental
conditions. Then, as an adaptive benefit, it was passed down
to his progeny.

If our response to environmental conditions can call forth
appropriate biological responses, what should be considered

the force that drives the species? Apparently a large part of it is environment.

Thus Lipton extrapolated that the source of "control" did not lie within the brain. Current research reveals that behavior is in fact driven by the environment. Organisms perceive the "environment" through specialized molecular sensors, which relay signals that select the appropriate software or genetic potential needed to make an appropriate "response." Biological organisms are complex "stimulus-response" mechanisms where the stimuli represent the environment and the responses are viewed as behavior. The sensors that interpret an environment and signal what is needed to the software or genetic potential waiting to be activated are what drives adaptation and change. This interpretation refutes the theories that purport only the brain as the interpreter of environmental data.

Feng shui is based on the same foundation as Lipton's discovery that an environment is a fundamental human motivator. To change the person, change the environment. The question of nature versus nurture is hardly new; however, perhaps we should see that a nurturer's input is also his or her particular response to the environment. Lipton's work points to a theory of interplay between nature and nurture. It is that fusion that drives, changes, and motivates us.

In a 1998 issue of *Architectural Record*, the editor, Robert Ivy, stated, "Read this twice, the subjects' behavior was more a determinant of their environment than their personality." The source is Roger Barker, renowned psychologist, whose work on human behavior is respected and longstanding. His work helps cement the realization that an environment is a far more powerful champion of successful personal experience than heretofore imagined. Consequently, the foundations of successful enterprises rest on perceptual evaluations, both explicit and implicit. We can stimulate the highest human potential by activating appropriate messages in an environment. What is put into place should not be taken lightly.

SELF-TRANSCENDENCE AND ENFOLDING ACCEPTANCE

In the hierarchy of needs, lower needs can be satisfied when higher needs are not. But it doesn't work the other way around.

In a workplace, attention to the foundational building blocks is a must if all are to reach their individual highest potential and also to be infused into the highest form of we-ness.

Self-Transcendence Experiences and Acknowledges All Processes

My father ran a jewelry manufacturing business, yet he never learned to be a jeweler, polisher, or stone setter. Although distant from the actual experience of the process, he was intrinsically aware of the process. He didn't have to actually learn how to move molten metal or bend a prong over a stone to be able to absorb what it feels like to do so, but being attentive to these processes without preconceived suppositions gave him the ability to "know" the process. The first stage of self-transcendence is experiencing and acknowledging all processes, especially those in which you are not directly engaged.

Self-Transcendence Relishes All Positive Experiences

Empathy is being able to imagine the subjective state around you, thereby absorbing and in some sense being the spirit of and in all. When all vibrations flow through us, nothing can shake, overwhelm, disgust, frighten, or be denied us. Until you personally dig a foundation, you will never understand how divine the breeze on the roof can be.

"Master," said the student, "where do you get your spiritual power?"

"From being connected to the source," said the Master.

"From being connected to the source of Zen?"

"Beyond that," said the Master, "I am Zen. The connection is complete."

"But is it not arrogant to claim connection with the source?" asked the student.

"Far from it," said the Master. "It's arrogant not to claim connection with the source. Everything is connected. If you think you are not connected to the source, you are thumbing your nose at the universe itself."

4

TAO, THE WAY
THINGS ARE

I s this a melodrama or your story?

Stuck inside, cut off from everything in nature, you are forced to remain within a three-foot-square space. Shadowless light glares overhead, and stagnant air recirculates through the entire premises. The sun will make its trip around half the circumference of the world without your basking in its warmth.

Throughout the millennia, societies have punished people with separation and isolation and rewarded them with inclusion and belonging. This process of connectedness or separation is the story of one Tao.

To begin your journey toward an improved work experience, it is imperative to consider the nature of the whole by examining the parts. In the same way that a jigsaw puzzle's pieces are not analogous to the whole picture until completion, many of us have only a partial picture of our own place of employment. When a veteran vice president of a large corporation failed to learn how to use a computer, he missed seeing the opportunity the Internet offered to enhance the company's image and sell products. It took his company years to catch up to an upstart competitor that ran away with a sizable portion of his company's market share. The segment that he did not know was the one that limited his effectiveness.

A similar story involves Amazon.com and the Barnes and Noble chain. An established bookstore chain, Barnes and Noble grew in numbers and size through the late 1980s and early 1990s until the Internet began to enter many households. With vision of a new opportunity, Amazon.com set up channels for distributing the world's largest book and music inventory without having the expense of owning the building and stocking the shelves. The rest, as they say, is history. After losing ground, Barnes and Noble followed Amazon.com's lead and began its foray into the World Wide Web. Being out of the loop seeds failure. Understanding the Tao is precisely how to stay inside the loop.

To see how you can produce positive work results consistently, examine your part of the whole. To discover where to seek support and how to produce better results, evaluate the entire process.

Another way of understanding the nature of a whole and its parts comes from Ken Wilber and Tony Schwartz's book *A Brief History of Everything.* A holon, the authors explain, is something that is a complete unit as well as a part of something else. A holon has two drives, wholeness and apartness, and this state exists in every facet of the universe, including your job. Consider the case of language. Spoken language is surely an independent structure and can exist without the written form. Letters too can exist as independent structures, but when strung together they form words, which include letters yet are an entity of their own. Words alone can't communicate complex thoughts as fully as sentences, nor can sentences alone be as informative as paragraphs. Ultimately using all these concepts, books covering a multitude of topics can be written, which up to now is the apparent end of this process.

Remove all the books in this world, and you will still have paragraphs. Delete paragraphs, and words will still survive.

Remove the notion of words, and letters will still be on the scene. Eliminate letters, and we will still be able to talk. Infuse language amnesia into a society, and we can grunt at each other. In other words, the lower processes are absolutely essential to developing the higher ones. Without support for the hierarchy, which evolves in any system, the structure will crumble.

The least prized, yet most necessary, unit is the one at the base, not the one at the top. The first expression of any unit is the one needed to support it. Even though we tend to esteem the most advanced or complex result, it could not exist without the support of the preceding levels.

Being in the Tao starts by knowing the process as thoroughly as possible. Courting exclusivity in the workplace is seducing disaster. What's below us affects us as surely as what is above. Without earth to absorb rainwater we would drown.

Here's a self-test to help you judge if you are in or out of the Tao of work. Answer yes or no to each question.

Test Your Tao Sense

1. Are you on a first-name basis with someone in every department?
2. Are you aware of the company's fiscal picture?
3. Are you cognizant of future projects in the planning stages?
4. Do you know the year the company was founded?
5. Could you mentally take the service/product through all the departments and/or stages it goes through before reaching its final form?
6. Can you confer directly with those immediately under/before and over/after your involvement?
7. Do you have some decision-making powers?

8. Are your personal needs or preferences generally met by the organization?
9. Have any of your suggestions been implemented in the last year?
10. Has any of your family visited your workplace?

If you have answered yes to more than eight questions, you are enmeshed in your organization's Tao. With this involvement you are likely satisfied with your role and a loyal employee.

Answering yes to between five and eight means you probably experience less than fierce loyalty. Most likely you keep an eye out for a new position and you would tell a white lie to get out of a company obligation.

With fewer than five yes answers, the likelihood of job satisfaction is diminished. It is in your and the company's best interest to reassess policies to establish an atmosphere of connectedness. Remember that belonging is a necessary ingredient to inspire the best and highest work, and being in the Tao implies enmeshment with your job.

The Tao also implies being connected to the physical surroundings in the same proportions as they exist in your reality. If you live in a rural area, nature's tapestry is essential to a workplace. This includes some elements of sound, scent, and air movement as well as a variety of line, form, light, and color. However, with few exceptions, rural settings include aspects of human culture. Be it through newspapers, magazines, TV, or the Internet; music, art, or the written word; even drama, dance, and concerts filter into the lives of those living close to nature. Therefore, human-made culture must be integrated in proportion to the observable or experiential signs in the surrounding environment.

In an urban setting culture's trademarks are theater, music, art, and fragrances of ethnicity. Those accoutrements may take the lion's share of Tao content in a physical space. Corporate art collections express the Tao of culture, as do those businesses that support local events. For those working in cities, being in the Tao implies having both natural and cultural realities incorporated into the workplace, with the balance tipped in favor of human-made elements.

Connecting to an entire office setting is an important Tao consideration. Where you are positioned in the entire layout impacts how you feel and how others feel about you. To be in the Tao is to be connected to all things in the physical world, all positive cultural contributions, and all processes underpinning what seems natural to you. Your enmeshment to the whole is not only what you do, but also where you are positioned in a structure, the amount of space you are allocated, the degree to which you can personalize your surroundings, and the belief that you have free, full access to the environment.

Here are thumbnail sketches of positions of office Tao and how others are likely to view you in each.

- The person closest to the room's outside entrance door is seen as the least essential component of a business and is often left out of the loop.
- The one closest to an interior opening or door may be assigned more work than others.
- The worker positioned in the center of a room is likely to be the mediator and a person relied on regularly.
- Those facing a wall can be considered inaccessible, and others may hesitate to engage them.
- Those with their backs to a window will not be listened to carefully.
- One facing a window often affords a sense of privilege and remoteness from others in shared space and will not be burdened by others, but may be resented.

While connecting to others implies being approachable and consequential, it is also important to establish an individualized presence. If you share an office, you may have experienced dashing back to your desk because you thought your phone was ringing only to discover it was a neighbor's. Merely distinguishing the ring of your phone from those around you can establish uniqueness.

Here are a few more simple ideas for establishing a singular presence in a sea of uniformity:

- If there is a uniformly designed nameplate on your desk, position it in a colorful block or on a small square of fabric.
- Keep fresh flowers or a plant nearby.
- Purchase a unique paperweight or letter opener.
- Place a felt square under a computer keyboard.
- Toss a scarf or square of fabric over the back of your chair.

Being part of the Tao doesn't mean obliterating your uniqueness. Just as there are many units building all processes, there are many units of Tao in your life. It is important to start at the beginning, which is you. Only when you have connected to your true feelings and talents will it be possible to connect to those around you. Start with yourself, your desk, and your office, and then you will be able to connect with others in the company. Those who have the largest circle of connections are often those whose imprint on life is most secure and manifest.

5

BALANCING ACT
The Yin/Yang of It

Y *in* and *yang* are words describing extremes. Hot-cold, big-little, and open-shut are simple ways of conceptualizing what yin and yang represent. Yin is associated with nonmovement, nonaction, silence, darkness, emptiness, stillness, and coolness, while yang is aligned with reaction, movement, loudness, brightness, fullness, activity, and heat. Ebbing and flowing like

Yin and yang

the rising and setting sun, the long, dark yin night recedes when the sun rises and begins its climb to the peak of the yang or the hot, active time of day. Midway between sunrise and sunset, the warmest time of any day is the exact moment when the sun begins its descent and the yang begins to fade, giving the opportunity for yin's darkness to begin its ascent. Yin and yang represent the cycle of life and contain all its possibilities.

Have you ever wondered why the classic yin/yang symbol has the small circle of white in the black area and the snippet of black in the white part? The peak moment of any extreme, like the

In every extreme exists the beginning of its reversal.

hottest part of the day, is when the change back to the other extreme begins. Thus, at the hottest time of day, we know that the slide toward cooler night is beginning.

Human biorhythms normally follow the same pattern as the rising and setting sun. We find the ascending yang of day (the morning) the time of intense accomplishments, peaking at midday, when activity levels wane like a shrinking moon. In the late afternoon, many discover their efficiency; energy and alertness have peaked.

This chapter will examine how yin and yang are manifested in our feelings and how to tweak an environment to enhance and support work. For example, if you need to concentrate, which is a yin characteristic, distractions of noise, movement, and interruptions will diminish competency. If clear, concise communication is required, feeling energetically yang can marshal sufficient energy. For example, live audiences are more stimulating to me than a TV camera, and preparation for an interchange is never quite the same as when the event occurs.

Certain adjustments to an environment can alter personality somewhat. However, a retiring, demure person cannot easily become a raging bull, and each of us is likely to function generally in either a yin or a yang mode. One state is not better or more productive than the other; however, some tasks are better suited to either yin or yang. The trick is to have a space lean toward the atmosphere that best supports your natural tendencies as well as the process in which you are engaged.

A yin atmosphere supports concentration and extricating ideas, and a yang atmosphere aids communication of ideas and marshals energy.

In addition to the activity's quality, your own natural place in the continuum of yin and yang needs to be considered. People too are either yin or yang in orientation. A salesperson is likely to be more yang than a research scientist. Compare the job requirements with your natural inclinations to discover whether the environment needs yin or yang adjustment. For example, an extroverted salesperson is not likely to be good at filling out detailed paperwork. Therefore, creating a yin desktop will help that salesperson function with greater ease, ultimately making the paperwork less onerous. Blending natural proclivities with that of the tasks will support better performance and diminish stress.

Take the following test to determine if you are predominately yin or yang. Circle the responses closest to how you would respond in a given situation. If there is a tie, choose two.

---

1. If you are at a table where two people start arguing, you will probably:

   a. listen intently and intercede with your analysis of the situation only when you can see the whole picture
   b. slide back in your chair and hope they won't ask for your opinion
   c. be able to hear the validity in both points of view no matter how heated the argument becomes
   d. agree or disagree after hearing only one person's point of view

2. You are asked to solve a human resource problem. How do you react?

   a. You listen carefully and mull over why the problem exists before you begin to think about its solution.
   b. You find yourself unable to express yourself coherently when tackling this problem.
   c. You are immediately engaged in thought about how to solve the problem.
   d. You jot it down and go right back to focusing on what you were doing.

3. How do you plan your day?

- a. Listing what you need to accomplish on a piece of paper buoys you.
- b. You have a hard time keeping up with what you have to do, finding even writing it down laborious.
- c. Scheduling tasks relieves any anxiety about accomplishing them.
- d. You don't take the time to write down what you need to do and feel anxious about whether you have remembered everything.

4. You are stuck in traffic getting to an appointment. Your first reaction is to:

- a. use the time to think about or make notes about a project you are working on and phone the contact to say you'll be late
- b. feel sorry for yourself that things always seem to go wrong and phone the prospect to say you're sorry but you will be late
- c. figure out a way to detour and race the clock to get to the appointment on time
- d. bang the steering wheel and seethe while making a call on your mobile phone to announce you will be late

5. You can't handle it when:

- a. you are given an order or assignment without explanation
- b. you feel as if someone is looking over your shoulder at your work
- c. someone is late for an appointment and doesn't call
- d. the pencil-tapping person you have been tolerating for years complains that your humming is annoying

6. When your work is criticized, you are likely to:

- a. feel happy that the faults were pointed out so that you can improve the work
- b. want to defend your point of view but are unable to find the words to do so

    c. see immediately what parts of the criticism make sense and what do not

    d. think that the critic probably doesn't understand the information and hurry to explain your position

7. When you feel bored with and tired of a project, you are likely to do which of the following:

    a. take a break and recharge your batteries

    b. feel bad about not feeling at peak

    c. go back to the assignor or another for a creative transfusion

    d. find yourself picking your cuticles, biting your fingernails, or engaging in some self-destructive habit as you keep on going despite your feelings

8. You have been headhunted by another firm and decide to take the job offer. How are you likely to approach your present employer?

    a. Wait for an appropriate time and share why you feel changing positions is good for your life's scheme.

    b. Struggle with how you will tell your employer that you are leaving and feel very uncomfortable doing so.

    c. Think about who in the firm should replace you and make this suggestion to your employer at the time you announce your leaving.

    d. Spring your resignation on your present employer or telephone in your resignation.

9. You become aware that your division is not doing well and that there might be cutbacks. How do you react?

    a. Look for a way to infuse your job into another department.

    b. Get caught up with worrying and find you are not keeping up with present assignments.

    c. Decide to speak to the boss about the ideas you have to reverse the downtrend.

    d. Decide to start looking for another job.

Both yin and yang exhibit positive and challenging characteristics. Evaluate the test by checking your answers against the following table. Notice that certain questions pertain to different aspects of performance. Your score can uncover your likely reactions to various situations. You may see a pattern emerging in these responses, or you may find that you fluctuate between yin and yang depending on the interaction.

After identifying your inclinations in a variety of situations, determine if your office, workstation, or desk is supporting your

Question # and Area It Affects	☯+ Yin Positive	☯- Yin Challenged	☯+ Yang Positive	☯- Yang Challenged
1. Human interaction	a.	b.	c.	d.
2. Human interaction	a.	b.	c.	d.
3. Time management	a.	b.	c.	d.
4. Time management	a.	b.	c.	d.
5. Emotional make-up	a.	b.	c.	d.
6. Emotional make-up	a.	b.	c.	d.
7. Emotional make-up	a.	b.	c.	d.
8. Creativity	a.	b.	c.	d.
9. Creativity	a.	b.	c.	d.

YIN +

Positive side of yin: inclination to calm, sensitive, creative, fertile imagination

YIN -

Challenging side of yin: tendency to get depressed and feel insecure, inability to articulate ideas or complete assignments

*Positive side of yang:
alertness, ability to think on
your feet, ability to focus in
any surrounding,
communicates easily*

*Challenging side of yang:
tendency to rush, tendency
to jump to the next project
before finishing the present
one, irritability, impatience*

work activities. If you are naturally yin and are performing yin tasks in a yang office, one with intense lighting, clanging phones, and chatty people, for example, you will encounter a great deal of strain and fatigue.

NEED YIN?

Yin spaces make you feel relaxed, self-absorbed, and able to focus inward. It is easier to concentrate in a yin space. Consider the normal human reaction in a library, usually a very yin space. Speaking in hushed tones, tiptoeing around, and taking extreme care not to bother others is normal protocol elicited by this yin space. Yin spaces allow us to contemplate and concentrate by offering little distraction.

Positive Yin Office Conditions

Variegated lights
Wood desks and padded chairs
Carpeting
Curtained windows
Concealed paperwork
Dark, muted colors
Orderly and clutter free

How to Add Yin Conditions to Cure a Yang Office Space

- Cover the desktop with a dark black cloth, blotter, or poster board. The color black represents the water element which relaxes and calms.
- Dimmer areas are yin. A desk lamp with a shade will cast a shadow, causing some parts of a desk to appear darker.
- Comfort is a yin condition. Place a small area rug under the desk. Be sure it does not interfere with a chair's mobility but is thick enough to provide a cushy feeling underfoot.
- Repetition is a yin feature. If desktop music is not an option, bring in a small clock, the kind that chimes at regular intervals.
- Focusing attention is yin. Bring in a clear crystal paperweight or any colorless object that refracts light. Refracted light helps you focus on the task at hand.
- Feeling tranquil is a yin condition. Dribble a few drops of a calming aroma like lavender onto a cottonball and place it near your chair.

Not all tasks require yin surroundings. When you need to communicate with enthusiasm on the telephone or in person, express ideas to a colleague, or take a break from concentrating, create a yang environment:

- Turn up the desk light wattage.
- Place a shiny or brightly colored paperweight on a desktop surface.
- Push aside any small rug or soft surface underfoot.
- Smell a sharp floral scent.
- Remove any faceted surface from the desktop.

NEED YANG?

Yang spaces make us spring to attention. They invite energy and excitement. When surrounded by a yang space, yelling or roaring with delight or dismay doesn't feel awkward. Feeling expansive and having options is a yang condition.

Positive Yang Office Conditions

Another workstation within voice
    distance
Overall bright lighting
Hardwood flooring
A blend of sounds like chimes,
    phones, voices, faxes, etc.
A physical feeling of abundance
Fresh, energetic scent
Bright, high-intensity colors

How to Add Yang Conditions to Cure a Yin Office Space

- Stack "in" boxes on your desk and arrange a row of reference books close by.
- Install a desk lamp to illuminate the entire desktop so no shadows are cast on its surface.
- Hard smooth flooring assists with ease of mobility, which is a requirement of yang.
- Add a variety of stimulating sounds on a computer or a desktop sound-producing device.
- Choose red, green, or orange reflective paperweights or desk items.
- Citrus scents, eucalyptus, clary sage, and rosemary energize by either removing obstacles or creating desire.

THE EFFECT OF TOO MUCH YIN OR YANG

Stress is imbalance. Be it physical, emotional, or intellectual, when pigeonholed or stymied from fulfilling our potential, the psyche rebels. Shutting down, not being able to think, or not caring to communicate or interact is indicative of an excess of yin, while nervousness, inability to concentrate, and inappropriate expressions categorize too much yang. Since we all have a unique proclivity toward either yin or yang, excessive stimulation in the direction in which we are naturally aligned could be detrimental to functioning.

To ascertain whether an environment leads you toward an extreme, focus on your feelings and how they affect your breath. In a yin atmosphere, your breath will naturally slow; in a yang atmosphere it will accelerate.

When bored, tired, or discouraged, notice that your breathing becomes shallower and shallower. As your breathing decreases in depth and pace, less oxygen is funneled to vital functions, causing continued decline. In a yin state, how we feel becomes highly exaggerated and important and interactions with the world become extremely subjective. It's as if the I becomes the total universe. "How do I feel?" and "How does this affect me?" and "How am I doing?" are questions that a yin state of mind produces. When completely yin, we can't see the proverbial forest because the only tree we experience is the one from which we peer.

When breathing becomes shallow, all systems slow down, as if they are trying to conserve energy for only the most essential functions. Essential functions are primal to survival so that when too yin you have little opportunity to focus on the emotional state of anyone but yourself. This can be a very unproductive mode for any employee. With too much yin an employee or a workplace is bound to be fraught with jealousies, self-centeredness, and detachment.

Do you function in a yin bubble?

Naturally functioning at optimum is a goal; therefore, when performance seems too yin, rev up yang in a work space.

On the other end of the spectrum, too much yang potentionally creates internal frenzy. The panting breath of fear is similar to yang's intensity. If you dread being late and find yourself feeling hysterical about meeting deadlines or talk compul-

GENERAL SIGNS OF YIN	HOW TO ALTER THEM TOWARD YANG
Too many shadows	Use overhead fluorescent or halogen lighting
White noise or silence	Add a ticking or chiming timepiece
Wall-to-wall carpeting	Add hard flooring under desk or in walkways
Sealed windows	Use a ceiling, floor, or desktop fan
No windows	Direct a small fan toward a lightweight material like a curtain, flag, or wall hanging

Yin Feeling	Possible Culprit	Cure
Disconnected	Not within voice range of another	Visit others at least a few times each day
Isolated	Empty areas or too much space	Warm up your office by covering empty surfaces with pictures or photographs
Unproductive	Too much overpowering office equipment	Interrupt sight line to large objects with a tall obelisk, plant, or flag
Shyness	Lack of wall art or air currents	Hang a clock with a pendulum on a wall

When an office is crowded with equipment, workers feel that they never can accomplish enough.

sively, you might be experiencing too much personal yang. Feeling yang also includes an intolerance for others or a tendency to anger quickly. Such conditions deplete focus. If you find yourself taking short gulps of air and you seem to be working harder and harder while accomplishing less and less, look for signs of too much yang in an environment.

When you feel undermined by others, it often helps to identify their behavioral mode. When someone is clearly yin or yang, adjust your own conduct to balance his or hers. This often produces a centering effect. When you encounter someone who exhibits the behaviors in the following table, consider applying the corresponding tactics.

Do you function in a yang bubble?

GENERAL SIGNS OF YANG	**CULPRITS**	**CURES**
No variation in lighting	Fluorescent overhead lights	Add a desk or task lamp
Too much activity	Too many people walking by	Screen desk area with a plant
Cluttered	Too many desks	Add citrus scent or reflective picture frames
Frenzied	Bright, fully saturated colors	Add dull, muted colors
Compulsive	Too many Post-its and papers	Cool down the temperature and turn on voice mail
Unable to listen	Too many items on desk	Add blue elements or curved artifacts
Feeling victimized	Lack of privacy	Add sentinels like a tall lamp or plant to edge of desk
Too bossy	Too much imposing furniture	Clear area around the entrance
Trying to sustain a false image	Work in progress is in drawers	Secure desktop "in" boxes

Our experiences in life cannot be separated from the language of our environment. No matter what our personality tendencies are, we react to a highly detailed vortex that, like drops of rain, pounds on our existence and becomes absorbed. Knowing yourself, others, and the stage on which they perform is a good beginning in the pursuit to understand how to benefit from feng shui's information.

Too Yang	Behavior in Another	What to do
Draws life force from others	Unable to listen	Be quiet
Tries to sustain a false image	Exaggerated self-aggrandizement	Agree with him or her
Perpetrator	Exacerbates confusion	Do nothing
Acts inappropriately bold	Sabotages work process	Refuse to be engaged in debate

Too Yin	Behavior in Another	What to do
Depends heavily on others' input	Defends the status quo	Continuously ask and wait for a reply
Denigrates work	Undervalues contributions	Agree with him or her
Victimized	Attracting trouble	Refrain from rescuing
Shy	Will not support the actions of others that agree with his/her convictions	Pounce on his or her good ideas

6

CHI FOR YOU

H ow vital do you feel? How much in life are you truly enthusiastic about? Do you wake up each morning awash in joy at the prospects ahead? The answers to these questions uncover the quality of positive chi in your life.

Chi is the expression of life. It takes every form and therefore can be positive or negative depending on what is needed to thrive in a particular situation. Positive chi can be fast and furious or slow and mellow, depending on what is needed to benefit the circumstances. Chi can be seen, heard, smelled, and touched. It can be expressed through words, actions, implications, all sensorial systems, and all physical content. We cannot extricate ourselves from inhaling the prevailing chi. One way or another, all things emit a message, and that message is the root of chi.

What messages flow forth from your workplace? Are these communications appropriate to progress, or does your environment thwart your effectiveness and contentment? Knowing the various expressions of chi and what messages are integral to a supportive working environment is the key to framing a positive work experience.

By examining the physical surroundings you can uncover the hidden messages of the environment. What you notice has the potential to be a benefit or a detriment to your work process. More often than not, the effect on your performance will parallel the amount of chi present.

If, for example, red, which is the fire element, is used in small increments throughout an office, then the influence that fire has on your performance will be moderate. The more vibrant and deeper the red, the more fire's reactions will be produced. If red is used in excess, the fire element's input will likely be negative unless the job requires an imbalance of fire, such as competitive sports, where the use of red in athletic uniforms can incite energy, rapid responses, and the mental animation to perform at peak. In an accounting office, in contrast, where attention to detail is required, the fire element could be distracting.

For most people, shiny surfaces tend to stimulate mental concentration. Therefore, when positioned by a computer whose operator needs to focus on the kind of minute details inherent in accounting, editing, or scientific research, shiny objects or surfaces can augment performance. However, too many shiny objects can hinder artwork, the drawing out of someone's emotions, or communication. Sparkling surfaces reduce access to emotions, which could be beneficial to someone fraught with an excess of uncontrollable emotion. Understanding the essence of the work and yourself is key in setting up appropriate office chi.

The qualities of chi can best be explained by understanding feng shui's five elements. All forms of chi—color, scent, touch, and sound—are expressed by the five elements. By assigning each sensory experience to an element, you can discern what element abounds in your workplace. Then it is up to you to look at the potential positive and challenging traits they encourage and decide if the element should be reduced or expanded to reap the best for everybody in the organization.

Once you determine the dominant elements in a workplace, review the emotional content that each element is likely

	COLOR	SHAPE	TEXTURE	DIRECTION	SOUND
FIRE	red/orange	triangular shapes	rough or highly textured	window facing south	loud occasional sound
EARTH	yellow/brown, terra-cotta, taupe	square shapes	solid, thick to the touch	desk in center of room	vibrations or repetitive beats of sound
METAL	reflective, white, silver, gold, or copper (beige or gray if shiny)	round or circular shapes	smooth	window facing west	high-pitched vibrations
WATER	black/blue	undulating or random lines	inconsistent surface	window facing north	unending or continuous undercurrent of sound
WOOD	green	rectangular shapes	grainy or prickly	window facing east	breathy, swooshy

Chi Is How We Experience the Physical Content That Surrounds Us

to engender. If there is a lack of an element's positive emotions, you might want to add some of the element that encourages that response. If you feel an excessive amount of an element's emotion and yet there is no representation of the element in the work space, you can balance the emotion by using the controlling element to reduce the excessive emotion. If, for example, you feel frenzied and yet there is no visible fire element, adding fire's controlling element or earth will dissipate the feelings of frenzy.

Charts A, B, C, and D can help with this process. Use Chart A to determine the amount of particular emotions present in your work experience, depending on your innate response to the environment. If your score is on the low end then your attributes are positive. If your score is higher, your feelings are potentially challenging. If you have a positive response, the amount of the element suits your needs. If your feelings are on the challenging

Chart A						
Rate the level of the emotions on a scale of one to five by circling one of the numbers.						
FIRE						
Enthusiastic	1	2	3	4	5	Frenetic
Keenly intuitive	1	2	3	4	5	Too subjective
Focused	1	2	3	4	5	Abjectly afraid of not meeting deadlines
Affectionate	1	2	3	4	5	Overbearing
Dramatic and vibrant	1	2	3	4	5	Abusive
EARTH						
Dependable	1	2	3	4	5	Inflexible
Practical	1	2	3	4	5	Rejecting of new ideas
Grounded	1	2	3	4	5	Stubborn
Responsible but not self-aggrandizing	1	2	3	4	5	Intrusive and self-serving
Loyal	1	2	3	4	5	Unrealistic expectations leading to disappointment

Chart A (continued)

METAL

Disciplined, able to concentrate	1	2	3	4	5	Unable to listen to others
Discerning	1	2	3	4	5	Continuously rejecting of suggestions
Upholding of highest standards	1	2	3	4	5	Anxious and strict
Respectful of authority	1	2	3	4	5	Blindly follows
Ritualistic	1	2	3	4	5	Compulsive

WATER

Visionary	1	2	3	4	5	Out of touch with reality
Imaginative	1	2	3	4	5	Exaggerates
Thoughtful	1	2	3	4	5	Oversolicitous
Truthful	1	2	3	4	5	Insensitive to others' feelings
Perceptive	1	2	3	4	5	Critical

WOOD

Independent	1	2	3	4	5	Intolerant
Adventurous	1	2	3	4	5	Impulsive
Inspires action	1	2	3	4	5	Causes havoc
Adaptive	1	2	3	4	5	Fickle
Focused until completing tasks	1	2	3	4	5	Self-punishing with too high expectations

side, it is better to reduce the amount of the element. Chart B can then uncover if the physical surrounding is empty or too full of the element attached to the emotion. Chart C will help you choose an element to support changes even if the original ele-

Chart B				

FIRE	NONE	SOME	MORE THAN OTHER ELEMENTS	CLEARLY DOMINANT
Red/orange				
Triangular shapes				
Rough or highly textured surfaces				
Windows facing south				
Loud occasional sound				

EARTH	NONE	SOME	MORE THAN OTHER ELEMENTS	CLEARLY DOMINANT
Yellow/brown				
Terra-cotta, taupe				
Square shapes				
Solid, thick to the touch				
Furnishings positioned in a room's center				
Vibrations or repetitive beats of sound				

Chart B (continued)				
METAL	**NONE**	**SOME**	**MORE THAN** OTHER ELEMENTS	**CLEARLY** DOMINANT
Reflective, white, silver, gold, or copper (beige or gray if shiny)				
Round or circular				
Smooth				
Window facing west				
High-pitched vibrations				

WATER	**NONE**	**SOME**	**MORE THAN** OTHER ELEMENTS	**CLEARLY** DOMINANT
Black/blue				
Undulating or random lines				
Surfaces of all heights and volumes				
Window facing north				
Unending or continuous undercurrent of sounds				

ment is not apparent in the environment. Chart D suggests some items and which elements they represent that can easily be integrated into a work setting.

Chart B (continued)				
WOOD	NONE	SOME	MORE THAN OTHER ELEMENTS	CLEARLY DOMINANT
Green				
Rectangular				
Grainy or prickly				
Window facing east				
Breathy, swooshy				

Chart B determines if the physical surroundings are empty or too full of the element attached to the emotion. It determines the dominant element in a space. Check the appropriate boxes.

A few colors don't fit precisely into the element categories. One is purple, which is similar to violet light and exists outside the visible spectrum. Because a violet wave of light cannot be seen by the naked eye, purple is associated with that which cannot be experienced directly or is otherworldly. It is not unusual for those in spiritual practices to gravitate toward purple. Psychics, palm readers, and practitioners interested in telepathy, auras, and other intuitive sciences will find that purple communicates their services better than other colors. When there is a need to tune into the elusive, nonconcrete universal consciousness, which may be the case in advertising, product development, future trending, or packaging, purple can be a supportive color.

When change is needed emotionally, use Chart C to determine how to incorporate the addition or neutralization of an element.

Chart C		

Fire	**Add**	**Remove**
Excessive Fire	Black (telephones) or blue	Green
	Matte finishes on major objects	Shiny objects
	Wooden accessories with curved lines	Monochrome rectangles
	Pale, undulating prints as chair cover or on windows	Vertical blinds
	Ambient music	Startling sounds

	Add	**Remove**
Lacking Fire	Red/orange accessories	Sight of blue
	Tall conical or rectangular objects	Blotters on desk
	Cuckoo clock	As many humming machinery sounds as possible
	Stacking boxes	Clutter

Earth	**Add**	**Remove**
Excessive Earth	Shiny objects	Excessive plants
	Round, conical accessories	Dark wood tones
	Triangular shapes or chevron patterns	Low, chunky furniture
	Bell on office door	Thumping sounds
	Cuckoo clocks	Lights creating shadows

Chart C (continued)

EARTH (CONTINUED)

	ADD	REMOVE
Lacking Earth	Change telephone sound to buzzers	Busy patterns on fabrics
	Terra-cotta pots	Chrome accessories
	Lower wattage in lights	Wheels on desk chair
	Carpeting under desk to rest feet	Chrome or gold pens

METAL

	ADD	REMOVE
Excessive Metal	Potted plants	White or beige file cabinets
	Landscape scenes	View of books or bookshelf
	Medium tones of blue and rose	Mirrors
	Fish tank	Ticking clocks
	Rotary telephone	Speakerphone

	ADD	REMOVE
Lacking Metal	Chrome or gold pens or yellow pencils	Dark-colored furniture
	Faceted objects in window	Heavy curtains
	Additional wattage	Shadows cast by desk lamp
	Circular frames or round wall objects	Square shapes on walls

Chart C (continued)

Water

	ADD	REMOVE
Excessive Water	Red/orange colors	Black or blue colors
	Vertical or horizontal blinds	Draped curtains
	Files or storage space close to desk	Clutter from desktop
	Freely rotating wheels on desk chair	Cushion on chair seat

	ADD	REMOVE
Lacking Water	Darkly colored artwork with undulating line	Hard-edged or linear artwork
	Nonspecific or unmatched shapes on desk	Dark blotters
	Wheeled files or office accessories	Harsh lighting
	Fabric window treatments	Vertical or horizontal blinds
	Winchester clock	Silence

Wood

	ADD	REMOVE
Excessive Wood	Small convex mirror reflecting only hard edged files	Sight of tall file cabinets
	Round framed pictures	Vertical rectangular framed art
	Draped fabric to window	Sight of red/orange
	Square carpet under desk	Any vertical pencil holders

Chart C (continued)	

Wood (CONTINUED)		
	ADD	**REMOVE**
Lacking Wood	Tall vase with fresh or dry flowers on desktop	Uniformity of accessories on desktop
	The color green in artwork or desktop accessories	Dark wood–colored accessories
	Striped fabric on chair or pad	Solid colors from desktop
	Lined notepaper	Pastel colors from computer screen
	Ticking clock	Square framed wall art

Chart D suggests items representing each element that are commonly found in office supply stores. Select an item from Chart D that you have an affinity for to introduce more of a particular element in your work space. Remember, no selection should in any way jar you, make you feel uncomfortable, or embarrass you.

In many ways, the quality of a workday is determined by how much of ourselves can be extended into a workplace. Although in most cases the self's extension is limited to the desk or immediate area around it, you can hang artwork on a magnet on a nearby file or frame a color or shape that sharpens or soothes you. Small adjustments can produce generous gains.

SOUND

Work sounds include silence, human voices, machinery, and music. The contribution of music to a work environment can

Chart D
Items Commonly Found in Office Supply Stores

FIRE	Red pens Triangular clocks Wastebaskets with handles Swivel and wheeled chairs Desktop accessories in a variety of heights
EARTH	Wood-tone accessories Ticking clocks Square wastebaskets Chairs with arms Square shapes for desktop accessories
METAL	Metallic accessories Round clocks or clock without numbers Cylinder wastebaskets Plastic pads for ease of movement under chair Rounded edges on desktop accessories
WATER	Black computer screen/telephone/pens Blotter on desktop Low round wastebasket Positioning of all desktop accessories on back of desk Office furniture without rounded edges
WOOD	Dark green blotter or pens Stacking rectangular wastebaskets of different sizes Roman-numeral clock Speakers positioned next to computer screen

be immense as long as attention is paid to how the tempo, type, and variety broadcasted merge with the kind of work and time of day. Even favorite foods can become boring, and perhaps distasteful, if no other choice is available.

Choose music that has the same energy as needed during that time of day. Wagner at 3:00 P.M. could add to flaring of tempers and perhaps depression, while Mozart at the same hour might uplift spirits and aid productivity. Too often music is selected only for its innocuousness. Here are some reasons why music in the workplace improves performance and why you should carefully consider the selection of music in a workplace. Don Campbell, in his popular book *The Mozart Effect*, expounds in depth about the effects of music.

• **Music affects body temperature.** Experiments have shown that great sweeps of sounds associated with striking the keys of a piano sequentially or a horn sound escalating from low notes up to the top note can raise body heat a few degrees. Who has not shivered with cold when hearing the high pitched grind of a creaky door? Who has not shuddered with distaste at the sound of chalk screeching along a blackboard? We shiver with one type of sound and sweat with another.

Use sound to help achieve comfort in places that may be too cool or too warm at different times of day. Many years ago I worked at a jewelry factory that was chilly on winter mornings. Had we had music with percussion and bass when we arrived, our personal thermostat would have heated up. Also, during the dog days of summer, light, detached, abstract music would relieve a sticky and suffocating atmosphere. Music helps us tolerate uncomfortable temperatures.

• **Music increases endorphins, and the brain's own opiates are activated.** Music that induces joy and emotional richness can help us feel generous, enthusiastic, and understanding. In Don Campbell's book *The Mozart Effect*, studies show that music activates production of endorphins that result in "feeling good" for no apparent reason other than the playing of certain kinds of music.

- **Stress-related hormones decrease with ambient music.** The phenomenon that stress-related hormones, such as adrenocorticotrophic hormone (ACH), prolactin, and human growth hormone (HGH), decline when ambient music is present has been reported by anesthesiologists. The dictator Lenin confessed to avoiding soothing music because he felt kind and did stupid things when that kind of music was playing. When stuck in traffic, the only way I can quell mounting anxiousness is to toss chamber music into my CD player.

- **Music can alter the perception of physical space.** In a crowded environment, music like Steven Halpern's *Spectrum Suite* adds dimension, removing a sense of clutter from a crowded place.

- **Music increases effective productivity.** In a study of copy-editing done at the University of Washington, a group listening to light classical music had a 21.3 percent increase in accuracy as contrasted to those listening to popular commercial radio, which improved in accuracy by only 2.4 percent. Music soothes the soul enough to improve performance significantly. Consider music a necessary ingredient in a work space to relax or energize you and to boost performance.

The factors that contribute to the energy or spirit of place include all information gleaned by our eyes, ears, nose, and skin and can be classified through the five feng shui elements. Therefore, you can hear fire, smell water, and taste wood while feeling metal. Evaluate all your senses to determine how messages are being transmitted in your workplace. When what you see, hear, touch, and smell aligns your energies with the best fulfillment of work tasks, your work space becomes a permanent ally.

PART II

ADJUSTMENTS

7

THE SCENT OF
SUCCESS

T he nose never sleeps, yet most of us are slumbering when it comes to being cognizant of scents surrounding us. We tend to notice only those fragrances that are particularly aromatic or pungent, yet aromas are the only sensorial experiences that penetrate a body's interior. Aromatics transport messages deep into our psyche, and when a physical location is devoid of an aromatic presence the sense of attachment is affected. It is beneficial to integrate appropriate scent into every physical location.

I remember the sweet scent my mother wore and how I could feel her presence when her closet door opened and the essence of Mom surrounded me. Every workplace and personal space should be associated with a fragrance that speaks of your presence and participation.

There is always the chance that a colleague or customer will dislike the scent you choose. No matter how commercially popular, a scent may be offensive to somebody. It may cause an allergic reaction or evoke an unpleasant personal memory. If, for example, a person's aunt, known for her caustic criticism, wore jasmine, then jasmine may trigger a disturbing emotional memory. Sometimes a co-worker might be avoiding you, being cool or distant, or even getting angry just because of a reaction to an applied fragrance.

One particular story of how fragrance reassembled negative memories was recounted by a friend at a recent gathering of executives in the fragrance industry. The woman's mother agreed to allow neighbors to plant a privacy hedge between their homes. As the hedge grew, becoming taller and thicker, so did her depression. Coincidentally, each spring after the hedge started to bloom, her mother's mood spiraled downward and she became increasingly depressed. By the time summer was in full bloom, so was her mother's immobility and despondency. Then, cyclically, as winter approached, her mother's mood would start reversing. When the last leaf had descended, life would begin to return to normalcy. Years later, when her parents migrated to Florida, her mother's cycle of depression vanished. Her daughter suspected that something in their childhood home had provoked the years of depression. This indomitable mother/daughter team finally uncovered the answer.

The privacy hedge's scent turned out to be an association she had when victimized in the concentration camps of Nazi Germany. Recalling the spring her family was ripped from their home and deposited in a death camp, her mother was able to remember that the very same hedge was in full bloom. Thus the last aromatic memory of home was the one that this hedge produced, and later in life her mental health went into a tailspin when the aromatic memory was triggered.

Not to diminish the power of our personal associations, certain scents, just like colors, exude universal qualities. Our common biological heritage has imprinted a story about each scent, and it is in our best interest to select one that telegraphs an appropriate message.

Scents, like the entire world's physical content, can be associated with the five elements. Consider which element works in your behalf and add it to a work area.

FIRE

 Fire scents promote intellectual acuity, competitiveness, enthusiasm, and quick responses. When we need a kick-start or motivation to complete a task, fire scents can be supportive. Use fire scents with discretion, however, because overuse causes extreme fatigue and depletion of energy.

 Scents That Increase the Fire Element

Lemon balm

Melissa

Rose

Ylang-ylang

Jasmine

Ginger

Laurel

Rosemary

Tea tree

When too many fire elements exist in an environment via red, add a triangular pattern or use an earth scent to reduce excessive fire.

 Scents That Reduce an Overabundance of Visual Fire Elements

Grapefruit

Cardamom

Fennel

Sandalwood

Geranium

EARTH

 When loyalty and reliability provide the best emotional context for a situation, the earth element has no equal. Just as feeling grounded when barefoot or supported when sitting on firm ground, earth element unifies and stabilizes an atmosphere. Use earth to support realistic goal setting, consistency, and steadfastness.

 Scents That Increase the Earth Element

Frankincense

Lemon

Sweet marjoram

Patchouli

Peppermint

When too many visual earth elements such as tan, brown, or terra-cotta, square shapes or patterns cause an atmosphere to be wrought with manipulation, stubbornness, and fear of change, employ a metal scent to dissipate it.

 Scents That Reduce an Overabundance of Visual Earth Elements

Cypress

Clary sage

Thyme

Juniper berry

Hyssop

Yarrow

METAL

 Discernment can be advantageous in business, when you must focus on and complete many tasks. Adding metal elements helps clarify what is important and what is not. Metal's virtues are perfect in a setting requiring analytical thinking, focus, and thoughtfulness. An office with a great deal of metal might not be a fun place to work, but a great deal of work will be accomplished. If your focus is on perfection, add the following scents.

Scents That Increase the Metal Element

+ METAL

Tea tree
Pine
Sweet marjoram
Eucalyptus

If jealousies and secretiveness abound in a workplace, mitigate these negative behaviors by reducing the metal element expressed by an abundance of shiny objects or the colors white, silver, and gold or patterns and shapes of a circle with earth. Earth conceals the overfocus and overseriousness of metal and brings a more realistic quality to an office.

There is another element that diminishes metal. Water, as represented by blue, black, and patterns with free-flowing wavy lines, elementally softens the edges of an environment with too much metal. So long as ailments are not caused by unhealthy environmental conditions, too many metal elements may be the cause of workplace headaches and illness due to strain and stress. Introducing a water element can reduce problems caused by too much metal.

— METAL

Scents That Reduce an Overabundance of Visual Metal Elements

Vetiver
Cypress
Geranium
Lemon
Benzoin
Red thyme

WATER

 If your business is human services, a water elemental scent can enhance emotional connections and underscore compassion. When flexibility serves a process, a water scent can be the catalyst to achieving it. Water's consuming and ethereal qualities invest an atmosphere with insightfulness and acceptance. Use water scents to increase the desire to nurture as well as maintian flexibility.

Scents That Increase the Water Element
Geranium rose
Juniper berry
Red thyme
Jasmine

When emotions run high or a major change is under way, reduction of the water element can be stabilizing and soothing. If you feel emotionally needy, temperamental, or critical, heap an atmosphere with elements of earth. When you feel your input will be rejected, shore up your emotional stability by reducing water's presence.

Scents That Reduce an Overabundance of Visual Water Elements
Sweet marjoram
Cardamom
Grapefruit
Coriander

WOOD

 Nothing serves the goals of business more seductively than the wood element. Wood's energetics and optimism for growth and change speak to expansion, leadership, an ability to thrive under pressure, and the willingness to endure. Elementally, wood imbues truthfulness in any situation because positive growth must incorporate realities. To imbue open-mindedness and a propensity toward growth and development, add wood.

Scents That Increase the Wood Element

Lavender

Bergamot

Chamomile

Peppermint

If you find yourself enmeshed in the pursuit of growth and change without regard for others or feel impatience and fault-finding erupting, you may be experiencing an overdose of the wood element. Too much wood can cause a feeling of being out of control, forgetful, and restless. When you demand from others more than you require from yourself, try curbing wood elements at work.

Scents That Reduce an Overabundance of Visual Wood Elements

Jasmine

Coriander seed

Ginger

Pine

Tea tree

Myrrh

Variety and edges are two other factors to keep in mind when bringing scent into a workplace. Life would be visually flat if all furniture, walls, paintings, and other elements in an environment were one color. If you would not play one song over and over, why would you infuse a space with only one scent? Just as we spice up other areas of life, choosing a variety of scents fills a workplace with the same rich sense of diversity as does visual variety. You know deep down that boredom rears its lusterless head without diversity.

A Variety of Places to Infuse Scents

Telephone

Use a cottonball to wipe these scents on the mouthpiece:
> Lavender to stay calm
> Thyme to help with decision making
> Lemon for clear, concise thinking
> Cypress to dispel fear
> Laurel for inspiration

Desktop

Put the following scents in a small dish or wipe them across your computer screen:

> Chamomile when patience is needed
> Peppermint to reduce overeating
> Yarrow to abate defensiveness and overprotectiveness
> Rosemary to boost confidence
> Tea tree to reduce the impact of emotional assaults

Threshold of a Room

Put these scents in a scent ball hung over the doorway or diffused in an electric dispenser:

Orange for compatibility and optimism
Melissa for fearless serenity
Coriander to infuse tranquil creativity
Bergamot to disperse stagnation

Just as walls define a room, every scent needs an edge. When a scent permeates ubiquitously, it loses effectiveness. Just as living without divisions between the bedroom, kitchen, play spaces, and work areas is not as appealing as having separate spaces, having only one scent in a space will not support your best functioning.

Here are the distances that scents travel:

Dispensed by wearing or applying directly—up to two feet
Dispensed by infusing in moving water—up to three feet
Dispensed by a heat element into the air—up to six feet
Dispensed by hot air projection system—up to twelve feet

Now you need only to begin to experiment. Start by trying a fragrance. Purchase only natural and pure ones. While they may be more sensorially seductive, mixtures do not punch the air with a precise message as does a solitary essential oil. I have found that John Steele upholds the highest standards in essential oils. Get his catalog by writing to him at 3949 Longridge Avenue, Suite F, Sherman Oaks, CA 91423.

8

THE BA-GUA

How Positioning Affects Productivity and Contentment

Perhaps I am excessively sensitive to being the odd person out because I reached my adult height at the age of ten. Always positioned at the end of any school lineup, I tended to feel ungainly, conspicuous, and unsupported. Position was key to my discontentment.

Do you feel happiest when surrounded by friends and family? Would you admit to feeling a bit out of the loop when stuck at the end of a row in a group photograph? Wanting to belong is so integral to the human experience that we often cannot find the source of our distress when placed at the perimeter of a situation.

Where are you positioned in the hierarchy of office space? It is well known that the newest person is likely to have the least-favored desk placement and/or locker, that the boss usually has a bird's-eye view of his flock, and that those in the center hold on to their jobs longer than do those at the periphery.

Position is quite revealing, and feng shui knowledge contains a great deal of information about the meaning of certain areas of a room or in a building. The position of your desk can affect your productivity, how others feel about you, and how you feel about your job. Learning the meaning of the positions in a work area can help you understand what might be helping or hindering your contentment and success.

Feng shui uses a tool called the *ba-gua*, which assigns meaning to different areas in a room. The designation is not selected randomly but developed from the rationales of human biological and physiological response systems.

The traditional pyramid ba-gua

Although the traditional Chinese ba-gua divides a space into nine areas, the pyramid school determines that shared business spaces have a reduced number of locations. The traditional ba-gua, like the one above, is useful to use for a private office or a home, but a group of co-workers, while they may be sympathetic to one another's needs, frequently have divergent responsibilities, hence goals. For that reason, the pyramid office ba-gua is a slightly different tool from the traditional one.

Traditional societies assigned more fixed protocols to each person and job. Inherent in this approach was the reality of an enduring social structure where the individual did not steer the course of her or his life in the same way we do today. When career flexibility became an option, when people began to change not only jobs but also careers, the parameters of the ancient ba-gua were no longer sufficient.

With the exception of one's personal desktop, in shared office spaces, the nine areas of the traditional ba-gua combine into five dominant forces. On a desktop, the nine different segments of the ba-gua are used because one single person controls that surface exclusively.

The ba-gua in shared offices

POWER AREA

The wall farthest from the threshold of a room is the power area. Power at work has to do with control, capability, and competence. A company's power is linked to the skills, intelligence, and stamina of its personnel, products, and services. When  the power area is endowed with these characteristics, a business will likely thrive. Thriving can refer to a variety of things: internal satisfactions of employees or external rewards such as receiving a raise, snagging a client, or meeting an important deadline.

The position farthest from a room entrance is the most secure. In fact, so ingrained is this position that it is most frequently selected for desk placement by those in charge. Part of your ability to advance in an organization is the perception of importance. Even if your desk is not farthest from an entrance, if you can screen it from direct view, others' perception of your power will increase. We tend to protect or hide that which we perceive as valuable. It stands to reason that valuables, be they people, papers, or icons, when placed in a protected location or where they are not easily visible, are imbued with authority.

> You are held in esteem if your desk is situated near the power wall facing the entrance to a space.

Positive Items in the Area Corresponding to Power Area

Desk, so long as the occupant
  sits facing the entrance
Growth charts and sales
  records
Icons suggesting future goals
Awards and achievements

What May Deplete Potency if Positioned in the Power Area

Desk facing away from the
  entrance to the room
Glass wall facing another
  work area
Coffee machine, water
  cooler, or general break
  area
Storage closet

ASSOCIATION AREA

"It's not what you know; it's who you know."
If that adage rings a bell, and if you feel as
if you have been overlooked for promotion,
perks, or incentives, consider the state of
workplace associations. The association area
is the right side of the room when you are
at the room's entrance. We tend to rely on, confide in, and trust
those we feel comfortable with. Placement in an office can

contribute to making you and others feel comfortable. What is positioned in the association area of an office suggests the comfort with or support for human interactions.

Do you know that you will be spoken to more frequently if you are sitting to the right of a person than if you were sitting to the left? If the lure of conversing with you is too compelling for a neighbor you can deter his or her frequent dialogues by changing a desk's position.

Human beings are dominantly right sided. Scientific research has unveiled that most left-handed people started life

> If the person with whom you are communicating has to turn to the right to listen to you, your input will be valued more than if the person has to turn to the left.

in the uterus as right-handed but underwent change during the course of prenatal development. Therefore, the comfort level for interaction is increased significantly when we have to turn, rotate, or circulate to the right.

If you want to be noticed at a meeting, sit on the right side of the decision maker. If you don't want to be given additional work, sit or stand to the left. Be it you or an icon, objects on the right side of a room will be interfaced with more frequently and noticed than those on the left. Have you ever noticed that when there are a few lines at a bank, the ones on the left are usually shorter?

Positive Items in the Area Corresponding to Association Area

Fax machine
Desk, if work involves
    communication or
    human services
Copier
Conference table
Reception area
Business plans or
    development ideas
Customer files

What May Deplete Potency if Positioned in the Association Area

Research or library area
Bathroom areas
Written dictates such as
    posted performance
    reviews
Awards or sales charts

MOTIVATION AREA

The area surrounding the threshold is the motivation area. Remember the first day on a new job? Perhaps you felt slightly overwhelmed and wondered how long it would take to learn the systems that seemed like second nature to other employees. What

motivates most of us at the beginning is the desire to learn and become competent. Do you feel the same way today? Do you hunger to acquire material that can propel you or your team toward expertise and growth? When there is a need to enlist motivation, evaluate what is present in the area nearest the office entrance and determine if what is there is inspirational. We at the Feng Shui Institute of America delight in seeing our membership grow. When we feel acknowledged in the public domain, the pressures of work seem to melt away. We keep a growing list of radio and television stations that have included information about our organization as well as laminated versions of articles in top-notch publications on the motivational wall. Seeing the fruits of our labor keeps us going even when the pressures of work seem to expand before our eyes.

If the corporate spirit seems to be waning, if you can't conjure up inspiration, it is time to rearrange, rehang, or reposition the motivational area of your office.

Positive Items in the Area Corresponding to Motivation Area

Desired rewards or
    goals
Reception area
Pictures of those who
    are admired in the
    industry
Inspirational books—
    such as *Feng Shui
    Goes to the Office*!
Files filled with resource
    materials

What May Deplete Potency if Positioned in the Motivation Area

Piles of unfinished work
Clock
Dimly lit area
Conference table

CHALLENGE AREA

The left side of a space is the challenge area.

Everyone has challenges to face. In fact, it is often the case that those areas in life that require our greatest attention also garner our highest achievements.

Because of my dyslexia, I am a slower-than-average reader. Reading and writing were the first hurdles I faced at school. In fact, I could not print or read until third grade. Since little was known then about dyslexia, I had to overcome its impediments by really listening carefully. As a reaction to being denied access to books early on, I became an avid reader just as soon as I was able to decipher the codes locked in the sequence of letters. What motivates us to pay attention is often what presents the greatest challenges.

Often life's peak experiences occur because we have stepped outside our comfort zone into unknown territory. Without challenges we are apt to atrophy and fall short of our potential. We read daily of people who have become heroes in the face of adversity. A triathlon competitor may never have entered the arena had he or she not become confined to a wheelchair.

Positive Items in the Area Corresponding to Challenge Area

Long-term goals
A place for
  contemplation
Inspirational books and
  publications
Printer
Computer

What May Deplete Potency if Positioned in the Challenge Area

File cabinets
Break area or coffee
  maker
Calendar
Scanner, copy machine,
  or other duplicating
  equipment

> If you love your job and feel accomplished at work, nothing is better or healthier than to place yourself in the center of the room.

CAREER VITALITY OR FINANCIAL HEALTH AREA

The physical center of an area or room is the survival or financial health area. What is your company's bottom line: information, sales, technology, or human resources? Whatever contributes to a business's health and stability contributes either directly or subtly to the financial health of a business.

The ultimate financial health of a business and your own career vitality may be, however, more complicated than that. While you may be reaping the rewards of sales, the company may not be adjusting to future exigencies with enough vigor to ensure ongoing success. No matter how well you do your job, your contribution is still just a segment of the whole, and assessing the vitality of the whole is important to your future. Knowing the overall fiscal health can be important to your future and current insights.

Positive Items in the Financial Health Area

Your desk, as long as you
    love your work
Central file system
Printers, fax machines, or
    other communication
    systems

Sculpture or life-
    enhancing features
    such as fresh flowers,
    water feature,
    terrarium, scent
    diffuser, etc.
Accounting or president's
    office

What May Deplete Potency if Positioned in the Financial Health Area

Empty receptacle for
  waste or shredders
Dictaphone
Vault or locked
  cabinet

Being able to interpret these five ba-gua areas enables you to meet both your own and the company's needs. Your boss may think you are a mind reader if you go into her or his office one day and announce, "I think we are having trouble motivating our staff" or "I don't think that we are carefully enunciating the company's challenges to our employees." Gaining understanding of potential problems before they get out of hand is one benefit of knowing how to read the areas of the ba-gua. Forewarned is forearmed.

9

FENG SHUI'S WORKPLACE GOLDEN RULES

F eng shui's concepts help to customize a work environment and can then be tailored to your particular desires and propensities. Start with the general rules that apply to most situations most of the time. When it is impossible to establish the classically ideal feng shui conditions there are always alternatives. Flexibility is what pyramid feng shui is all about. In this chapter, then, I offer feng shui's golden rules for the workplace, plus some viable options when you simply can't follow the rules to the letter.

Twenty Golden Rules

1. Face a room's entrance when seated at a desk.
2. Make sure there are no pathways behind a desk chair.
3. Position your desk so that it is not directly in line with the entrance to the room.
4. Illuminate all the pathways seen directly from your work position.

5. Direct light to shine over your nondominant hand.
6. Put materials used most frequently within reach or within one roll of your chair.
7. Adjust your chair height so your work is at comfortable eye level.
8. Position the phone on the side of your desk at your dominant ear, not your dominant hand.
9. Put inspirational articles in clear view.
10. Shelter your personal space.
11. Be sure your desk area can be converted into an appropriate communication space.
12. Be sure your work area engages all five senses in some way.
13. Surround yourself with colors that answer your needs.
14. Create a clean, clear work space.
15. Keep a live plant in your office and maintain it.
16. Use plants to clean airborne toxicity.
17. Position electrical outlets so you don't have to crawl around on the floor to reach them.
18. If you desire change, relocate twenty-seven items to other locations.
19. Personalize the piece of office equipment that you use most frequently.
20. Organize your work space at the end of each day and keep surfaces free of dust and grime.

1. FACE A ROOM'S ENTRANCE WHEN SEATED AT A DESK

It is imperative to feel fully at ease and completely safe when concentrating. Our survival instincts are never asleep, and whenever we feel at all vulnerable, a part of our concentration is distracted and subconsciously focuses on any sounds, shadows, and vibrations that might indicate we are being approached.

If You Can't . . .

- Purchase a convex mirror and position it to reflect the entrance door.
- Mount a sound-producing item on the door like a door harp or bell looped over the knob.

2. Make Sure There Are No Pathways Behind Your Desk Chair

It is distinctly unnerving to have someone walk up from behind. Again, we are programmed to be on guard if we feel our backs are exposed and therefore vulnerable.

If You Can't . . .

- Place a convex mirror on a surface facing the direction of the traffic.
- Shield your workstation with a screen, a plant, or some object that feels like a wall or barrier.
- Position a highly reflective object in a location that will draw a passerby's attention away from you.

3. Position Your Desk So That It Is Not Directly in Line with the Entrance to the Room

If your desk is directly in line with the doorway, you will frequently be the first person asked to carry out a task and most likely be expected to accomplish more than your fair share.

The best course of action is to move your desk to deflect the attention lavished on those seated directly across from an entrance door. This is especially important to parents who work at home. You are already a target for your children's attention; don't ask for more.

If You Can't . . .

- Place a highly reflective or faceted object on the left side of the desk with the right side of the object facing the person entering the work space. Refracting light captures the eye's attention, and just so long as the object isn't a direct reminder of you, visitors will be distracted and tend not to focus on you.

4. Illuminate All the Pathways You Can See from Your Work Position

I recently gave a slide presentation to a corporation's top leaders. After the presentation when the lights were turned up to full brightness, I realized that I had failed to make eye contact with one woman, who was wearing an outfit the same color as the wall covering and had dark hair and complexion to boot. I missed connecting with her because I could not see her clearly. It's not hard to understand the importance of being able to identify easily all who come to your workstation. We all feel more open to helping and cooperating with those who immediately acknowledge us and remember our names.

If You Can't . . .

- Hang a cloth or poster with a great deal of bright yellow on the wall. Objects have greater clarity against yellow, and the contrast will improve the chances of a person entering your space getting your attention.

5. DIRECT LIGHT TO SHINE OVER YOUR NONDOMINANT HAND

Don't settle for an environment lit solely by overhead fluorescent lights. Only barren terrains have light without shadows. Place the desk light on the side of your nondominant hand so that shadows do not form on the work surface when your dominant hand is in use.

> Task lighting positioned over your least dominant hand provides a shadow-free, and therefore inherently distraction-free, work surface.

If you are right-handed, lighting should come from the left; if left-handed, from the right.

The area of your visual focus needs a shadow-free light source.

If You Can't . . .

- Purchase a yellow pen or pencil to write with. Yellow focuses attention and can somewhat mitigate shadows.

6. Put the Materials You Use Most Within Arm's Reach or Within One Roll of Your Chair

Picture yourself as a commander at the epicenter of mission control. If getting supplies or going to frequently used office equipment seems annoying or interrupts the work flow, rearrange the available space at your desk to include those items you need to stay in the flow. If, for example, you have to interrupt printing out a report to go to another location to select the correct paper, you may want to reduce the other papers at your workstation to accommodate more variety. It takes far less time to organize the location to house the necessary equipment and supporting documents than to go get what you need throughout the day. What is used daily must be within easy reach.

If You Can't . . .

- At the start of each day, anticipate tasks and place needed items close by or on the desk.
- Use your gofer trips as opportunities to stretch and get your circulation going. Any physical movement is a health benefit.

7. Adjust Your Chair Height So Your Work Is at Comfortable Eye Level

During my early computer days, I experienced terrible eyestrain. My bifocals made me tilt my head at an unnatural angle to see the computer screen clearly. Finally, I figured out that even though my desk chair could not be raised high enough, a pillow on the desk chair would raise me to the proper height. Take time to adjust your work space to achieve a comfortable eye level. Even the smallest annoyance can, over time, affect output negatively.

If You Can't . . .

- Use the lower half or upper half of the screen, whichever is appropriate for your eye level. Better to have a smaller screen than muscle pain or eyestrain.

8. POSITION THE PHONE AT YOUR DOMINANT EAR, NOT YOUR DOMINANT HAND

Many people place their desk phone on the side of the dominant hand without considering which ear they tend to listen with. Since far more time is spent listening than dialing, locating the telephone on the dominant listening side is reasonable.

Phone should be placed at your dominant ear.

If You Can't . . .

- Purchase an extension cord to elongate the telephone's wire and move it appropriately. I have been told by very smart people that they keep their phone on the inappropriate side because the cord is not long enough. They feel particularly embarrassed when I point out that the investment of an extension cord is typically under $5.

9. PUT INSPIRATIONAL ARTICLES IN CLEAR VIEW

If anyone else could occupy your desk without having to remove any personal desktop items, you have not created a place that embodies your uniqueness. If your desk is as impersonal as a motel room, think about making it reflect your uniqueness.

If You Can't . . .

- If company policy prohibits desktop adornments, customize your computer's wallpaper screen or screen saver with family photographs, landscapes, or patterns that speak to your soul.
- If policy prohibits change of screen savers, place postcards, photographs, or other personal visuals inside your top desk drawer, where they will come into view whenever you retrieve necessary items throughout the course of a day.

10. SHELTER YOUR PERSONAL SPACE

Having no private space can be intimidating and unnerving. A plant or screen higher than your seat can provide a sense of privacy essential to maximum proficiency.

In a shared space, make sure there is adequate partition or uniqueness of space separating each person from the others. I cannot stress the importance of creating a sense of privacy, especially if your workstation is close to another. Feeling safe from intrusion and competition goes hand in hand with producing the highest and best outcome. Not to dismiss the importance of competing, but even a marathon jogger whose performance during a race is energized by the crowd frequently trains alone. Being observed is beneficial just so long as the shared experience is sandwiched in between periods where you can be alone.

If You Can't . . .

- Stack "in" boxes in a location that hides your immediate work area from passersby.
- Fashion a screen with a sheet of foam core, readily purchased at any office supply house. Score and bend the ends as indicated in the drawing, and secure it with tape to the edges of the desktop.

Having at least a partially concealed space on a desktop can create a secured personal niche, which is essential in generating self-esteem and personal power.

11. Be Sure Your Desk Area Can Be Converted into an Appropriate Communication Space

Natural to most processes is communication. Space to exchange ideas, discuss procedures, explain results, or socialize is usually advantageous. By understanding what type of seating encourages different communication styles and attitudes, you can arrange your desk area to accommodate each situation.

Metal Seating

Any seating that approximates sitting around a round table imbues a situation with the metal element. Because authority is not invested in one person due to a unique seating position, all parties tend to assume responsibility for the process and

Metal seating ensures that verbal exchanges and ideas will flow and those around the table will be experienced as equally valuable.

invest maximum effort into finding solutions. Metal seating encourages verbal exchanges.

Wood Seating

A long rectangular boardroom table is ideal when decisions must and should be made. Wood seating encourages decision making and assuages fear of being innovative. When the majority of people are sitting side by side, intimacy is diminished because few verbal interchanges take place between people sitting adjacent to one another. Short, brief, to-the-point kinds of conversation are likely when the majority of people are sitting side by side.

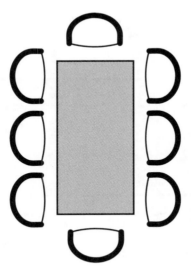

Rectangular tables create wood seating, which encourages decision making and prevents fear of innovations.

Fire Seating

When authority needs to be vested in one person, fire seating is preferable. Fire seating places one person facing all others. A lecturer in an auditorium is the quintessential example of fire seating. However, I have seen this arrangement used incorrectly by professionals who should be seen as allies to their clients. For example, marriage counselors, interior designers, architects, and others who are cocreating with clients should not use a fire seating. In that position the pressure is on the one in the isolated seat. If decisions are best made in conjunction with a client, avoid a fire arrangement. When you want to or should be in control, the fire configuration provides an appropriate platform.

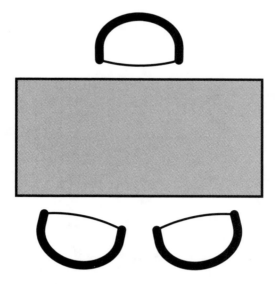

Fire seating, any configuration where one person is at the apex of a triangle, imbues that person with all the power and responsibility.

Water Seating

When feelings need to be expressed freely or when the goal is to acknowledge everyone's input, water's random seating pattern is best. Without a set pattern, we are confronted by our feelings. When established modes aren't reinforced, we are challenged to decipher how to act. In situations that call forth the need to adapt to heretofore unknown criteria, people tend to view each other as allies working through a crisis.

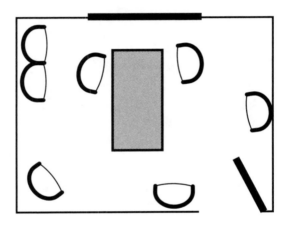

Water seating is random and nonspecific. It ensures heartfelt communication.

Earth Seating

Only groups of four or eight persons can comfortably be seated in an earth configuration. The shape of earth is a square because the feeling of earth's seating is stability and respect for each person's participation. In an earth seating arrangement no one person faces more or fewer people than anyone else.

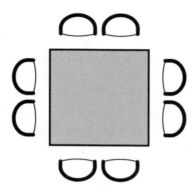

Earth seating evokes a feeling of belonging and security, and is created when seated around a square.

If You Can't . . .

- If positioning chairs around a desk or table is not an option, position them around an area rug or square floorspace.

12. BE SURE YOUR WORK AREA ENGAGES ALL FIVE SENSES IN SOME WAY

Spending most of the day indoors means being sequestered from our daily Arcadian rhythms. Arcadia was a remote area of Greece where people lived solely according to their biological and daily patterns. They awoke when the sun's rays scanned the earth's surface, ate when hungry, and wound down all activities after the sun dipped below the horizon. Like most premodern people, the Arcadians lived in sync with nature, and we invoke their name when speaking of being in touch with the natural biological rhythms of life.

Humans were meant to live outdoors and developed sophisticated sensors over thousands of years with which to take in information. Therefore, when humans began sequestering themselves indoors for most of the day, the full use of the senses was denied. Aside from visual information of line, form, and color, offices are often bereft of a variety of sound, smell, and touch. Be sure to have something to smell, feel, and hear that is appropriate to the energy needed.

If You Can't . . .

- Purchase velvet, satin, and pile cloth to drape alternatively over the edge of a desk, arm of a chair, or under a mouse pad. Your wrist is particularly sensitive and will give you awareness of different sensations as you touch the cloth throughout the workday.
- Purchase a Winchester desktop to add auditory variety throughout the day.
- Cottonballs scented with different aromas stored in zip-top plastic bags can personalize your work area. (See Chapter 7, "The Scent of Success.")

13. SURROUND YOURSELF WITH COLORS THAT ANSWER YOUR NEEDS

What if an office decor is not appropriate for your particular emotional needs? (Refer to Chapter 6, "Chi for You" to determine how colors affect the subconscious and what positive or negative feelings might be evoked for you.) If there is a disparity between what you need and a workplace color scheme, here are a few suggestions:

Use the complementary color on your desk to neutralize a color that you find incompatible with your work requirements. For example, if your work requires a high energetic state and the office's color theme is blue, place an orange fabric or poster board under your mousepad, writing station, or telephone.

- If blue is incompatible, use orange.
- If orange is incompatible, use blue.
- If red is incompatible, use green.
- If green is incompatible, use red.
- If yellow is incompatible, use purple.
- If purple is incompatible, use yellow.

14. CREATE A CLEAN, CLEAR WORK SPACE

All work areas must be clear and clean. Yes, that includes the desktop or any drawer opened at least once a day.

If You Can't . . .

- Throw away postcards you've been saving because they are pretty, unlabeled floppies, your umpteenth AOL free disk, a bank receipt from six months ago, half-used writing pads, desktop gifts that embarrass you to display, a leaky pen, or any item you have not touched in three months. Drop them into the nearest wastebasket. Remember you need only one bottle of Wite-Out, one roll of Scotch tape, one box of paper clips, one supply of stapler refills close by.

   If you can't force yourself to throw them out, change the location to a more remote area or alter the way you keep them.
- Clean up material stored behind any open door. I know the intention when placing things behind a door is to store items there temporarily. How long is

temporary? I have a routine that is pretty easy to follow: on the first of every month, temporary becomes permanent, and I have to either act on what I've kept behind the door that day or store it in a more appropriate place. Items hidden behind doors only signal that we are unable to handle our workload. Moreover, when a door cannot be opened flush against the wall, over time, those entering feel blocked, stymied, and frustrated. Blocked entrances are metaphors for actualization impediments.

- Eliminate unnecessary objects inside tightly packed filing cabinets. The best way to lose 20 percent of office fat is to perform a seek-and-destroy mission inside this piece of office furniture.

- Set up a regular cycle like the first day of each season to check files in use and remove any documents that are duplicated or no longer necessary. This routine can halve a file's thickness.

- Place the most frequently used files in the cabinet closest to your work area. If a file has not been used during the last month, it is probably safe to relegate it to a more distant cabinet. Files, reading materials, and papers should be pertinent to projects and be within a short walk (three to five steps) and within convenient sight.

15. Keep a Plant in Your Office and Make Sure It Is Healthy

Often the state of plants corresponds with the state of the owner. When plants are drying out, so are ideas. When plants are taking over your workplace, you may have outgrown your job. Keep a plant in your office and know that its health parallels yours.

16. USE PLANTS TO CLEAN TOXIC AIR

Fresh air is a rare commodity in many offices. Toxins that are exuded from plastics, inks, and other surface materials can be leaching into the air you breathe. Plants can absorb some of these toxins. If you experience frequent headaches, sleepiness, or unusual irritation, consider installing one of the following plants.

Plants That Eat Formaldehyde

Formaldehyde is used in many carpet glues and furniture made from pressed woods. Check the labels.

> Boston fern
> Chrysanthemum
> Gerber daisy
> Date palm
> Bamboo palm

Plants That Eat Ammonia

Ammonia is found in many cleaning supplies. Check the labels.

> Lady palm
> King of hearts
> Lily turf
> Lady Jane
> Chrysanthemum

Plants That Eat Benzene

Benzene is in fumes from new paint, also found in cleaning fluids. Check the labels.

> Gerber daisy
> Chrysanthemum
> English ivy
> Snake plant

Plants That Eat Xylene

Xylene is a solvent used in paints and varnishes. Check the labels.

Areca palm
Dwarf date palm
Dumb cane
Dragon tree

General Poison Eaters

Peace lily: ammonia, benzene, formaldehyde, xylene
King of hearts: ammonia, formaldehyde, xylene
Lady Jane: ammonia, formaldehyde, xylene
Weeping fig: ammonia, formaldehyde, xylene
Tulip: ammonia, formaldehyde, xylene
English ivy: ammonia, benzene, xylene

17. POSITION ELECTRICAL OUTLETS SO YOU DON'T HAVE TO CRAWL AROUND ON THE FLOOR TO REACH THEM

The amount of wires and equipment used on each desktop boggles the imagination. Electrical wires looping behind a desk often look like the snakepit in *Raiders of the Lost Ark*. Aesthetics notwithstanding, the ordeal of sorting out which wire belongs to what machine while crawling around the floor hardly contributes to executive feelings or image.

If You Can't . . .

- Purchase an outlet strip and mount it on the wall or secure it on the backside of a desk. While the need to plug in equipment is not a regular daily occurrence, the daily look behind a desk will be improved.

- Roll up long wires to be sure that none touches the floor. Long wires cascading in every conceivable way add to the appearance of chaos, which does not enhance a feeling of organization and tranquility.

The old adage that we must be in the right place to actualize new ideas or opportunities is rooted in the reality that the ways we handle places we have control over reveal our basic approach to life. When working with space we are also working with our emotional makeup. To be clear and consistent, as well as able to perform at optimal levels, we need a space that parallels our aspirations.

18. IF YOU DESIRE CHANGE, RELOCATE TWENTY-SEVEN ITEMS IN A WORKPLACE

Change is a blend of letting go of old ways and incorporating new ones. My friend Debby returned from a trip to Montreal brimming with news that she bought out the clothing stores because the value of our dollar was so strong compared to the Canadian dollar. She justified her apparently outrageous number of purchases by intoning, "I meet clients all the time and just can't wear the same things over and over." But, she couldn't fit all of her new goodies in her closet. What a dilemma, I sympathized. I offered to help her by taking some of her old clothes off her hands. New things require letting go of old unused ones.

Whether it's work clothes or promotions, there has to be a readjustment, sorting out, culling, or freeing of old stuff before the new comes in. The adage "ring out the old, ring in the new" is one to keep in mind.

Why twenty-seven items? In traditional feng shui, the number twenty-seven is suggested to prepare the way for change. When pondering why this would be a good number for pyramid practitioners to suggest, I realized that it has both substance and eccentricity. Not a familiar ten or twenty things, but a rather large, yet not overwhelming number of things to attend to. Change is not easy, and this separates those who truly want it from those who merely dream about it.

If You Can't . . .

- Toss away any office supply that is either rusted or grimy from disuse.
- Rearrange your desktop to be more efficient. That alone can produce about a dozen changes.
- Shift the location of a wastebasket.
- Rearrange the paper on a bulletin board.
- Go through a desk drawer and rearrange and consolidate the items inside it.
- Exchange one wall-mounted artifact with another.

19. Personalize the Piece of Office Equipment That You Use the Most

Does one piece of office equipment dominate your work life? I stare at my laptop for most of my working hours. How dreary it would be if my laptop did not have a stamp of my individuality. What message are you sending yourself if you have not taken time to nourish yourself with an affirming "I am"? Be it a telephone, computer, or adding machine, your window to self is expressed by customizing a piece of office equipment that embodies your work effort.

If You Can't . . .

- Download a favorite painting for your desktop screen.
- Peel and paste all sorts of shapes around the equipment's border.
- For a festive occasion, attach a balloon to a piece of equipment.
- Stick just about anything lightweight and appropriately sized on a surface with two-sided tape, which can be purchased at any office supply store.

20. Organize Your Work Space at the End of Each Day

How long does it take before you become slack about mess and clutter? No matter what the time frame, the fact remains that it is easy to become oblivious to our own clutter. Usually not until a client visits your work area or a meeting is scheduled in your office or around your desk do you look at the surroundings with "new" eyes and begin cleaning up. We develop a blind spot for our own clutter, but that does not mean it does not affect our performance.

If You Can't . . .

- If you look straight ahead to a sea of Post-Its, a grimy window, or a blank or uninspiring wall, remember your subconscious is receiving negative signals. Why remind yourself that you are apt to forget to do something (Post-Its), that your aesthetic needs really don't count (blank wall), or that you don't care or don't prioritize spending energy to keep an environment clean.

Inspire yourself, write affirmations, find a calendar, picture, photograph, poster, or three-dimensional icon that represents your core values. Don't just push-pin it in place but frame it with a favored wood, gilded, or high-color frame or mount it on a poster board in a chosen color to inspire you. You become what you see, so gift yourself and do whatever it takes to make your work area pristine and pleasing.

Free yourself from encumbrances and paraphernalia. Simple adjustments can make a work space not only more efficient and comfortable, but also more likely to help you achieve the clarity to embrace your dreams.

10

Desktop Magic

When Control Is Limited to a Desk

T he only control most of us have of our work space is the desktop. This area becomes a microcosm representing not only our entire world but also the way we feel about our work. What is placed on a desk and where it is placed can expose a great deal about what we like to do and what we'd rather not have to do. Understanding how placing items on certain parts of a desk can augment a work process, support individuality, and make daily tasks increasingly pleasant can help us achieve greater satisfaction and reach our goals.

According to the stories about feng shui in the popular media, by merely locating a plant or a symbol in a specific area of a room, we can be promoted or find true love. If only it were that simple. Alas, luck notwithstanding, most of us experience good things when we work toward a goal and have clear, unimpeded intentions that guide us down a self-actualizing path. A job transforms into a dream career when we have built a solid foundation to support our talents. In other words, we achieve our heart's desire when we are ready and can focus on those conditions that help make them a reality.

For many, the roadblocks to accomplishment are self-imposed. We don't trust our own ability to shape our destiny and won't dare beyond the boundaries of comfort to chance the unknown. Only by testing ideas can we make giant leaps.

My father helped me understand that without failures I would never be successful. It might, he wisely admonished me, take five or six misses to get one hit. Successful people are those who dare to try and are not fearful of failure.

By observing your desktop your desire to take risks can be discerned. What icon is present which is slightly removed from what is considered mainstream in your industry? What projects await you that are self-generated? How have you dared to go beyond what is considered protocol for your position? The following examples may indicate a person who is ready to walk the extra mile:

- Two Rolodexes
- Phone headset or other piece of office equipment that is not required for the job
- Unusual reference books
- Tape recorder
- Thought-provoking personal icon

The ba-gua as laid out in Chapter 8 applies to rooms in an office. Here we will return to the pyramid's nine-area ba-gua for the desktop, because this area is under your control. It represents you specifically and reveals you more complexly and fully. Each section resonates with an important life area. Why these areas are positioned in specific ways is not magical or mysterious. Under each section heading I will explain why these concepts are aligned according to a precise pattern. The following illustration is a map of the sections as applied to any space and used here on a desktop.

There are no accidents of placement. On a subconscious level the placement of any object reveals what a person feels about his or her own talents and the work at hand. Without an understanding of the ba-gua, cryptic messages are camou-

Traditional ba-gua

flaged. Our own and others' intentions are astonishingly transparent with a knowledge of the ba-gua.

What does it take to attain a goal? First, a goal must be clearly conceived. Stating "I want to make more money" is clear, but the way to achieve this is not specific enough to engender success. Identifying special talents that help you attain success is a more lucid way to think about setting goals. Once you have decided how to proceed toward the goal, you can use feng shui techniques to help the process unfold. Ascertaining what would help you achieve that goal is the first step.

Here's an example to follow to help you reach your goal.

A. Goal: I want a raise.

B. What do I need to do to achieve my goal? Increase sales.

C. What qualities can increase sales? Energy, communicating with greater precision, feeling more confident.

D. What elements should be selected as colors, icons, or shapes to help me reach my goal?

E. In which areas of the ba-gua should these elements be placed?

A, B, and C are questions you have to pose and answer. Question D can be answered by using the following chart. Finally, the remaining part of this chapter will reveal the answers to question E: where to place these objects on the desktop.

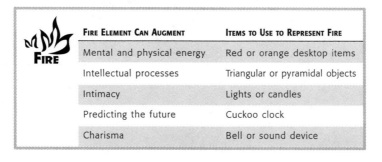

FIRE	**FIRE ELEMENT CAN AUGMENT**	**ITEMS TO USE TO REPRESENT FIRE**
	Mental and physical energy	Red or orange desktop items
	Intellectual processes	Triangular or pyramidal objects
	Intimacy	Lights or candles
	Predicting the future	Cuckoo clock
	Charisma	Bell or sound device

EARTH	**EARTH ELEMENT CAN AUGMENT**	**ITEMS TO USE TO REPRESENT EARTH**
	Peaceful solutions	Terra-cotta or color of the earth in your desk accessories
	Confidence	Square objects
	Negotiation	Crystal, rock, or shell
	Loyalty	Heavy, squat, nonshiny paper weights
	Security	Earthenware pottery

METAL	**METAL ELEMENT CAN AUGMENT**	**ITEMS TO USE TO REPRESENT METAL**
	Clear communication	Shiny, silver, gold, copper, or reflective desk items
	Concentration	Circular or round desk accessories
	Organization	Metalic desk accessories
	Ability to see through subterfuges	Clary sage– or eucalyptus-scented paper
	Ability to control	Metal sculpture

WATER	**WATER ELEMENT CAN AUGMENT**	**ITEMS TO USE TO REPRESENT WATER**
	Staying powers	Blue or black desk accessories
	Seeing the truth	Wavy-lined patterns on desk items
	Imaginative resources	Water feature or glass vase
	Honesty	Moisturize or vapors from hot drinks
	Empathizing	Water-theme desk calendar

WOOD	**WOOD ELEMENT CAN AUGMENT**	**ITEMS TO USE TO REPRESENT WOOD**
	Being a pioneer	Green desk accessories
	Meeting a challenge	Tall rectangular desk items
	Accepting change	Grainy wood box
	Taking action	Tall plant
	Continuously developing	Rectangular framed free-standing artwork or mirror

In our example, the elements that help to increase sales would be fire for energy, metal for communication, and earth for confidence. The next step is to place these elements in the area of the ba-gua that needs enhancing. Fire energy should be placed in the relationship area, for what else are sales calls but building strong relationships? Metal for communication stands to benefit in the wisdom area of the ba-gua. Feeling confident is a way of shoring up one's personal power, which is represented by the self-empowerment area.

At the end of each section of the ba-gua are suggestions for the right symbol to use for each element. Pick one and place it in that area of your desk to give you the subconscious message in the appropriate areas. For our example, the desktop would be configured in the following ways:

Fire: a red object in the relationship area to promote energy for sales calls

Metal: a scent diffuser with clary sage in the wisdom area to augment communication

Earth: a terra-cotta pencil holder placed in the self-empowerment area to increase confidence

Sophia had returned to work after a fifteen-year absence. She wanted desperately to be able to succeed in the normal business community. Although the job called for a communicator/salesperson, the main tasks involved meticulous attention to detail and timetables. She could think on her feet and liked to have a variety of verbal challenges, but since she had been absent from the work world for such a long time her knowledge of and familiarity with technology and paperwork were rusty. Consequently, over the course of a few months, the piles of papers waiting to be entered on her computer's database swelled exponentially, and she moved them from their original position on the right side of the desk to a place underneath the desk. She repositioned the telephone from the mid-right side of her desk and placed it directly in front of her. These two simple changes communicated her desire to ignore tasks she felt less capable of doing and augment the one she liked. It became obvious that she focused on telephone tasks rather than the paperwork.

Since many of us don't control the entire office, attention to placement and choices on a desk or workstation in relation to the ba-gua's information can help us define our own challenges as well as talents.

When change is desired, shifting attention to more productive or essential tasks can motivate us to change.

The following actions would help Sophia reprioritize her responsibilities. By adding three "in" boxes on the far left of her desk labeled "Today," "This week," and "This month," Sophia would begin to have a handle on the lag in her paperwork. It would lessen the amount to do by sorting it into time frames, thereby making the amount of entry work less daunting. By placing the computer on the near left side of her desk, she would have it close at hand but not in the position of her dominant side, which would cause her to feel as if this task was easy. By making a task that we do not like to do manageable and placing it in a position that corresponds with the reality of how we feel about the task, we are giving ourselves permission to acknowledge which tasks are arduous. I would further suggest that she plan a consistent time frame each day, either early morning or the end of the day, to enter a prescribed amount of data from the oldest "in" box. If she moved the telephone to the close right side, it would still be convenient and would free empty space in front of her desk chair, which would balance her desk and her feelings about the two tasks.

1. Computer

2. Telephone

3. Printer

4. Fax Machine

5. Picture of Loved Ones

6. Rolodex

7. Pens and Pencils

8. Pads of Paper

9. "In" Boxes

10. Desk Lamp

11. Empty Space

12. Cluttered Space

The Desktop Dozen

Please note that even if you have control over an entire room, it is important to read this chapter to uncover your feeling about work tasks. Both what is potentially positive and what is challenging are discussed in each ba-gua section.

Only you know if the message that the item emits is helping or hindering your progress and contentment at work. The beauty of feng shui and the use of a ba-gua is that a physical change initiates the inner change. Just as a sign over a door saying "All those who enter are blessed" can help those who use the space feel special and appreciated. The subconscious message telegraphed by objects on a desk either subvert intentions or fulfill them.

Start reading your desktop ba-gua by sitting or standing in your customary position. The spot where you first perceive, encounter, or activate your work area is the position from which you will read the ba-gua. Normally, a chair is positioned in the bottom center of the desk. In each area of the ba-gua, the "desktop dozen" will be discussed along with how the placement of the particular item relates to the position being discussed.

SELF-EMPOWERMENT

The self-empowerment area is located at the top-left-hand corner. How you feel about a field or job or if you're on track and doing work that is aligned to your spirit can be observed by what objects are placed on the far left side of a desk. The self-empowerment area is filled not only with symbols of our talents

Self-empowerment area— far-left-hand side

and desires but also frequently with representations of personal work-related goals.

Julie Kroll, who runs the Feng Shui Institute of America, has placed her overflowing "in" boxes in that area. Her cherished goal is to be able to empty them. Her strength is that she can tackle the innumerable details it takes to run a professional organization and sort them out so that she gets done what needs to be done. Her personal business power and value is her ability to effectively juggle her work's disparate details.

The far-left-hand side of a desk typically has items that people feel imbue them with power or with those objects that express their talents. For example, awards, recognition plaques, and other signs of achievement are often hung in this position in a room. Placing them there connotes one's feelings of satisfaction with what the icon indicates has been accomplished. The choice of tools placed in this powerful position can expose your level of self-confidence as well as those things you fear.

Begin by evaluating the desktop dozen. As with all content, there is a potential for the message and meaning to be either positive or challenging. Uncovering why you choose to place items in particular positions on your desk can reveal what you need to focus on or improve or what should be additionally nurtured and supported.

> The far-left-hand corner of the desk describes how you feel about your talents and abilities to perform at work.

What each object may be communicating when placed in the self-empowerment area:

Computer

- Positive—You likely experience work generated on the computer as the tool that catapults you ahead.

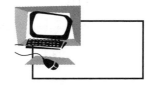

Computer in the self-empowerment area

- Challenging—You do not feel as if your true brilliance can be expressed by what you generate on the computer. Perhaps you would be happier if you could verbally express the ideas or simply do the task rather than have to write about it.

Telephone

- Positive—You are likely to feel effective as a communicator and feel an affinity and talent for verbal expression.

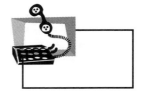

Telephone in the self-empowerment area

- Challenging—You see verbal justifications and the sale of ideas, projects, or products as a necessary evil. You find the need to justify your work difficult.

Printer

- Positive—The written word is your ally and office memos are your favored means of communication rather than face to face meetings. You place much

Printer in the self-empowerment area

value on the written word and feel comfortable with that talent.

- Challenging—You feel overwhelmed by the amount of written communication necessary and are likely to edit work endlessly.

Fax Machine

- Positive—You value a constant stream of information and welcome challenges from elsewhere to hone personal power. You can defend your way of thinking without feeling put upon.

Fax machine in the self-empowerment area

- Challenging—You feel encumbered by others' input on the job and would welcome more autonomy.

Picture of Loved Ones

- Positive—It is the network of loved ones with whom you are intimately involved that gets you going each morning. Your life centers on family. It is their love that steers your life course.

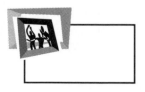

Picture of loved ones in the self-empowerment area

- Challenging—You may feel that without your family you would not survive. You may feel guilty about the lack of time spent with them.

Rolodex

- Positive—You are a
  consummate networker,
  one who needs to keep a
  paper record of contacts
  in this age of computers.
  You know the value of
  others to your career
  development.

*Rolodex in the self-
empowerment area*

- Challenging—You are a
  collector who is more involved in the chase than in
  fortifying the structure. You may feel as if advancement is in the hands of others and your fate is not
  directly in your control.

Pens and Pencils

- Positive—Positioning
  writing implements on this
  side is positive only if you
  use pens ceremoniously, to
  sign letters, documents, or
  checks. Placing them out
  of easy reach brings
  fanfare, pomp, and

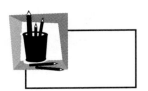

*Pens and pencils in the
self-empowerment area*

  circumstance to their use. The pen's brand and cost
  indicate your self-confidence level. Are you a Bic or a
  Mont Blanc?

- Challenging—Since most of the human race is right-
  handed, placing implements of communication on the

left side indicates an insecurity about your personal worth.

Pads of Paper

- Positive—Although you may not write often, when you do, you expect others to follow. Others rely on you. You are very likely in charge or will be soon.

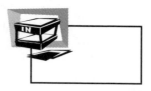

Pads of paper in the self-empowerment area

- Challenging—You tend to worry a great deal about what you write. You are the type that fusses over each letter, reading it over and over again to make it as perfect as possible. Whatever leaves your desk must be accurate and reflect precisely what you mean to express.

"In" Boxes with Work or Just Piles of Work Papers

- Positive—When times are tough, you will roll up your sleeves and get the work done. Determined to complete each project with excellence, you are likely a perfectionist.

"In" boxes in the self-empowerment area

- Challenging—The reports, letters, or written materials it takes to complete a job interfere with what you really like to do—namely, think up ideas and generate action.

Desk Lamp

- Positive—You take full responsibility for garnering knowledge to become successful at what you do. Hard work is a friend.

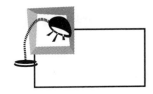

Desk lamp in the self-empowerment area

- Challenging—If wishing could make it so, you would wish to be more productive, come up with more innovative ideas, and become a leader at work.

Empty Space

- Positive—You are so secure in your own ability to rise to any occasion that no symbol is necessary.

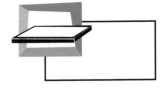

Empty space in the self-empowerment area

- Challenging—Feeling successful is as elusive as underwater-breathing. It is hard for you to see your own value, and you often don't take the credit that is your due.

Cluttered Space

- Positive—Overflowing with talent and confidence, even the prospect of unending challenges will not impede your self-confidence.

Clutter in the self-empowerment area

- Challenging—You feel as if the weight of the world is resting on your shoulders. You often feel powerless to change a negative situation into a positive one.

Items to Place in the Self-Empowerment Area

Fire—to bolster confidence: a red
    accessory
Earth—to help you feel secure: a square
    object
Metal—to increase your focus on meeting
    goals: a shiny article
Water—to quell self-doubts: a black or
    navy blue undulating shaped object
Wood—to encourage a positive self-
    image: a green leafy plant

FUTURE

We worry mostly about what will or will not happen in the future. We worry about getting sick, and when we are sick we worry about not getting well. Adults worry about the safety of their children, and teenagers often worry about having friends or obtaining good grades. What you have placed in the future area of a desk—the back center edge—can represent what you are fearful of or uncertain about.

Future area—the center of the back area of the desk

What is placed in the center at the far edge of a desk
reveals secret worries or the area of life you need to focus
on to achieve success.

Computer

- Positive—If a job has many
  facets, yet most time is spent on
  a computer, the positioning of
  the computer in the future area
  may indicate awareness of the
  need to clear space for the other
  tasks. If most of a job's tasks are
  generated on a computer, then
  you likely feel confident in your ability to perform well.

*Computer in the
future area*

- Challenging—Placing the computer directly in front
  but slightly out of reach indicates a reliance on, yet
  slight insecurity about, what is generated on the
  computer. Knowing how important computer-
  generated work is to your successes leaves you little
  choice but to use a tool that you feel cannot
  completely display the full measure of your talent.

Telephone

- Positive—You are shrewdly
  aware of the need to communicate and connect with
  those at work. A telephone is
  placed in this position to avert

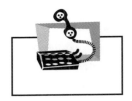

*Telephone in the
future area*

myopia and secrecy and to keep avenues of
communication open.
- Challenging—Escape might be a way to deal with
details. Someone who can mentally quit the job by
secretly playing games on the computer might also
keep a phone in this position and use it to
squander time.

Printer

- Positive—You can formulate
and articulate ideas well.
Understanding that your
concepts are pertinent to job
success, you are able to keep
ideas flowing and know that
they directly influence the

*Printer in the
future area*

company's bottom line. Those who place a printer in
this position know that their finished work is integral
to a company's survival.
- Challenging—Indicates a great deal of insecurity about
finished work. Nothing leaves your work space without
being edited extensively, or else you will not feel secure
about what is produced.

Fax Machine

- Positive—You have a finger on
the pulse of your industry
and easily communicate well
with all its facets. Unafraid to
be challenged, you keep
abreast of all new innovations.

*Fax machine in the
future area*

- Challenging—Needing approval from others, you seek
support from outside sources before sharing ideas.

Picture of Loved Ones

- Positive—You have a mature understanding of the lives of those you love. Not likely to engage in reckless behavior, you are a caring sibling, parent, or spouse and possess awareness of how to interact appropriately in the lives of others.

Picture of loved ones in the future area

- Challenging—Fearful of not providing or being able to give support to loved ones, you see responsibilities to them as a roadblock to personal contentment.

Rolodex

- Positive—You have a great deal of confidence in your ability to network and value the people you become acquainted with or wish to connect with.

Rolodex in the future area

- Challenging—You rely far too much on opinions of others and don't trust your own ideas and decisions unless backed by others.

Pens and Pencils

- Positive—You are confident and effective in communicating, which is the key to your ability to endure crisis and change.

Pens and pencils in the future area

- Challenging—Rarely used pens and pencils located in future's area indicate a desire to exude confidence in areas that you feel deficient in.

Pads of Paper

- Positive—The number of ideas you have is boundless, and your confidence in producing them ad infinitum is unwavering.

Pads of paper in the future area

- Challenging—Fearful of not being inventive, you may downplay the need for a change of procedures. You may suffer from writer's block.

"In" Boxes with Work or Just Piles of Work Papers

- Positive—Being able to go through heaps of material is your forte. The knowledge that a job depends on your ability to complete work is gratifying. It is important to be a significant contributor at work.

"In" boxes in the future area

- Challenging—Fearful of not being able to do a job properly, you feel slightly hysterical about completing tasks competently and may burn the midnight oil frequently.

Desk Lamp

- Positive—Self-reliance is high on your personal agenda. As Harry Truman said, "The buck stops here," and you completely agree with that adage. You assume total responsibility for what happens.

Desk lamp in the future area

- Challenging—You put far more pressure on yourself than is required, often adding others' workloads to yours.

Empty Space

- Positive—You have a healthy attitude about what might happen in your future and deal with circumstances as they arise without a great deal of anticipatory anxiety.

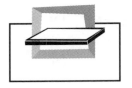

Empty space in the future area

- Challenging—Feelings of not having much control over what unfolds at work create apprehension.

Cluttered Space

- Positive—With bountiful options and diverse interests, life is never boring.

Clutter in the future area

- Challenging—Feeling overwhelmed or out of control, driven by endless demands and an inability to delegate responsibilities, is exacerbated by an inability to take charge and make decisions based on thoughtful consideration.

Items to Place in the Future Area

Fire—to spark focus on today rather than worrying about the future: a pyramid desk object

Earth—to help you focus on present issues: a Rubik's Cube

Metal—to increase concentration to garner long-term results: a clock in a round case

Water—to banish nail-biting anxiety: a Winchester clock

Wood—to help maintain the impetus to secure results: a tall rectangular container

RELATIONSHIP

What is placed on the far-right-hand side of your desk reveals what or who motivates you. Who your most important ally is at work and what drives your commitment are often symbolically visible in the relationship area of the ba-gua. Human beings are not naturally

Relationship area— far-right-hand side

solitary, and the value placed on relationships with others is often related directly to personal contentment. A great deal of what we do revolves around communicating ideas. For that reason the way others feel about us can ultimately promote or sabotage our work.

Although many people have photographs in the relationship section, it is just as common to place something that symbolizes what revs their engine. My sister is a theatrical producer responsible for selecting plays and working with playwrights.

> The motivator for success is visible by what you place on the far-right-hand side of the desk.

It is not at all strange that she has positioned her desk lamp on the right-hand side. Communicating without appearing critical is the ball a producer must juggle to extricate the best from those that drive artistic success. Light symbolizes clarity and perfectly expresses the valuable asset in my sister's work.

In the workplace it is not a given that relationships will be with people. Relationships with time, talent, techniques, or results are often expressed in this area. My friend Deborah, owner of a large employment agency, always keeps a plant, real or artificial, in that corner of her desk. It is interesting to observe that the times when the real plant has died usually coincide with the times she has confronted roadblocks to growth. Deborah feels her value to her company is her ability to keep its volume and income expanding. A downturn threatens her. When her attention is turned to reversing her company's downward trend, she is able to care for her live plants and typically removes the artificial ones. It is interesting to note that the company's fortunes seem to parallel the health of the plant in the relationship area of her desk.

Computer

- Positive—The computer is an indispensable tool, which may successfully translate what you do. You find it hard to imagine how you were able to get things done efficiently before computers. If you have grown

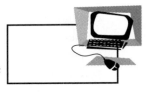

Computer in the relationship area

up with computers, you think of them as an extension of self.

- Challenging—Time is eaten up by the necessities of data entry. Tasks such as keeping a day planner current seem more laborious on a computer than in an appointment book. Resentment builds for those processes that formerly were done manually. If only your work didn't center so much on the computer, you believe job satisfaction would escalate.

Telephone

- Positive—You are your company's lifeline and feel confident in the ability to communicate its message effectively.

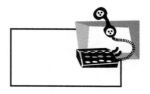

Telephone in the relationship area

- Challenging—The daily thorn wedged in your side is to have to explain or justify your performance to others.

Printer

- Positive—You are confident in your ability to create action, harmony, and relationships by exercising your talent as a communicator. The written word expresses you more exquisitely than verbal communication.

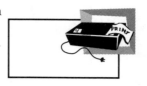

Printer in the relationship area

- Challenging—You feel more comfortable with ideas than people.

Fax Machine

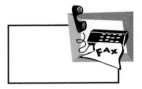

Fax machine in the relationship area

- Positive—You feel confident as a spokesperson for your company and love to telegraph its image and products to the world.
- Challenging—It seems as if you are always waiting for bad news to arrive, and are often insecure that you are not quite up to date on what's current in your industry.

Picture of Loved Ones

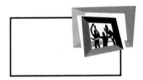

Picture of loved ones in the relationship area

- Positive—Your priorities are with your loved ones. Placing photos in this position helps to keep a proper balance between home and work.
- Challenging—You place photographs in this position so that those who enter will be unaware of your feelings of guilt over the lack of time spent with loved ones.

Rolodex

Rolodex in the relationship area

- Positive—A great deal of power is in your hands because of the networking you have cultivated. Over time the attention you have paid to keeping these connections alive has most likely paid off handsomely.
- Challenging—Lacking confidence in your own decisions, you feel compelled to run ideas by others before bringing them to the table.

Pens and Pencils

- Positive—Confident that your work is a great asset to your company, you take great pleasure in submitting ideas for any business undertaking.

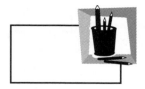

Pens and pencils in the relationship area

- Challenging—You might be overly critical of others' original work and feel compelled to improve on what they have done.

Pads of Paper

- Positive—The company's successes are integrated with your self-esteem. When work is running smoothly you can feel sublime.

Pads of paper in the relationship area

- Challenging—A great deal of fear surrounding your ability to continuously produce creates anxiety that you will not be able to come up with the next "good" idea.

"In" boxes with Work or Just Piles of Work Papers

- Positive—You are a paragon of responsibility and can be depended on to perform to your maximum capacity.

"In" boxes in the relationship area

- Challenging—Work is a substitute for other gratification. The expression "all work and no play" applies to you.

Desk Lamp

- Positive—The ability to sort out what is important helps work excel. No task or project is undertaken without a great deal of thought as to the best way to proceed.

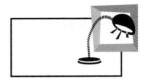

Desk lamp in the relationship area

- Challenging—Feeling more than your share of responsibility for successes at work, indecision inundates you when trying to determine what is the best course of action. This leads to being unable to make a timely decision.

Empty Space

- Positive—Possessing clarity and charity toward others at work, you are able to think clearly about how to improve human relationships in the workplace.

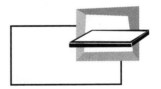

Empty space in the relationship area

- Challenging—You may avoid dealing with co-workers. If you don't get along with your boss, an empty relationship corner indicates you may not have figured out how to improve this situation.

Cluttered Space

- Positive—You are brimming with enthusiasm and ideas. Work energizes your life.

Clutter in the relationship area

- Challenging—You are caught in an unrelenting cycle of work, work, and more work. Never feeling caught up, you feel guilty when you are not engaged in work-related activities.

Items to Place in the Relationship Area

Fire—to pare down stressing about emotional attachments: a jasmine-scented candle

Earth—to help sustain long-term connections: a rock paper weight

Metal—to be able to penetrate emotional clutter: a mirrored box or container

Water—to help build belief in your on-target emotional instincts: a black telephone

Wood—to support adventure outside self-imposed limits: a green plant

DESCENDANT

Who doesn't desire to leave a legacy? How sweet to know your contributions will be integral to others and pertinent long after you are gone. In the same way as our biology drives us to get our gene pool into the

Descendant area— mid-right-hand side

next generation, the emotional desire to be significant to business successes is strong. The center of the right side of a work space is known as the descendant's domain. The consequence of our contributions motivates us to succeed. Your wish for a positive legacy and what you do to manifest it can be ascertained by examining the descendant area on the desktop.

> Our contributions to future successes encapsulate the descendant area's essence.

The right-hand side of the room represents all types of relationships based on the right-side dominance of the human race. Although many of us don't articulate our wish that our life's work be significant in the future, much of what we do is based on achieving that goal.

Scott, a bank trust officer, keeps his Rolodex in the descendant area of his desk. Since one important part of his job is to attract customers to his bank, his placement of this cache of people in the descendant area perfectly represents his desire to promote this process.

What is placed in your desk's descendant area indicates your depth of understanding of a business's vital signs. Further, what you place in this area divulges the talents you deem most valuable in the long run.

Computer

- Positive—Possessing a healthy creative vein, you communicate it through this piece of equipment.
- Challenging—Fearing a creative block, you spend far too much time working and reworking the jobs that call for innovative intervention.

Computer in the descendant area

Telephone

- Positive—Possessing the gift of gab, you are comfortable communicating and delegating ideas to enhance work for which you are responsible.

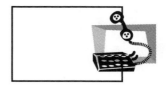

Telephone in the descendant area

- Challenging—Feeling insecure about transmitting ideas, you rely on others to challenge and overhaul your ideas.

Printer

- Positive—Trying fervently to keep promises, you want others to feel they can rely on your attention to communicating ideas in a forthright manner.

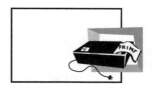

Printer in the descendant area

- Challenging—A master of verbal manipulation, you often feel uncomfortable expressing a forthright opinion.

Fax Machine

- Positive—With a deep security in your immense talents, you comfortably use them for the benefit of whatever you are working on.

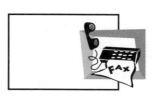

Fax machine in the descendant area

- Challenging—Depending far too much on others for inspiration, you often cast aside your own ideas in favor of others'.

Picture of Loved Ones

- Positive—You are richly
  rewarded by the impact
  you have on those you
  love. In fact, knowing
  that they benefit from
  your talents is a source of
  great satisfaction.

*Picture of loved ones in
descendant area*

- Challenging—You have
  confused making money with supplying the
  necessary requisites for those you care about.

Rolodex

- Positive—You give gener-
  ously of your time and
  talent to customers and
  business colleagues and
  are generous in sharing
  information.

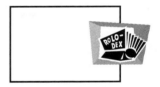

*Rolodex in
descendant area*

- Challenging—Feeling
  threatened by the accomplishments of others, you are
  driven to keep abreast of what others are achieving.

Pens and pencils

- Positive—Letters, memos,
  and E-mails are some of
  your favorite ways to
  communicate ideas and keep
  in touch with others.

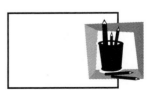

*Pens and pencils in
descendant area*

- Challenging—Expectations
  of your own output are
  exceedingly high. Be careful to recharge your
  creative juices.

Pads of Paper

- Positive—You are never at a loss for ideas. Creativity flows like water from a faucet, tapping an unending series of ideas.
- Challenging—You are at a loss to express yourself verbally to those with authority over you.

Pads of paper in descendant area

"In" Boxes with Work or Just Piles of Work Papers

- Positive—Thriving under pressure, your creative juices flow best when you have many projects to work on.
- Challenging—Putting immense pressure on yourself to perform, you can be your own worst taskmaster.

"In" boxes in descendant area

Desk Lamp

- Positive—Possessing confidence, you are eager to have your performance scrutinized by others.
- Challenging—With a tendency to blame others for failures, you are likely to be blind to the benefit of altering your performance. Flexibility is not your strongest suit.

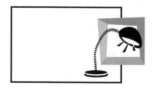

Desk lamp in descendant area

Empty Space

- Positive—Eagerly awaiting each challenge, you are confident in your ability to handle whatever comes along.

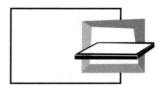

Empty space in descendant area

- Challenging—Not making waves is your attempt to camouflage yourself and avoid being assigned additional tasks or singled out.

Cluttered Space

- Positive—You are undaunted by a multitude of tasks, and your output is astonishing.

Clutter in descendant area

- Challenging—Overwhelmed by diversity of responsibilities, you are likely to turn in work behind schedule.

Items to Place in the Descendant Area

Fire—to feel assured that your creativity will sparkle when needed: pyramid object

Earth—to augment security when making creative decisions: earth-tone ceramic tile object

Metal—to reveal untapped creativity: reflective or gold globe-shaped object

Water—to lessen anxiety about splitting your time between family and work: water feature, such as a fish bowl, small fountain, or glass vase with draping vines

> Wood—to support a decision to alter a relationship
> blocking growth: tall cylinder filled with pens and
> pencils

COMPASSION

Compassion toward others can be
the fulcrum that supports business successes. Although many
tasks are solitary, the way you
present ideas to others determines
how your contributions will be
received and integrated. With the
support of others you will find
your proposals and inspirations
greeted appropriately.

*Compassion area—directly to
the right of desk chair*

> What is placed in the compassion area of a desktop
> displays your ability and desire to be empathetic
> toward co-workers.

The compassion area of a desktop telegraphs how you feel
about others. When others come into your workplace, the item
or items placed there will reach and grab their subconscious
with the message of your capacity to be empathetic.

Compassion means "with passion," and this is not an area
for subtlety. The clearer and simpler the symbol, the more
acutely your compassion will be communicated. Regula, my
literary agent, has to discover authors whose talents she believes

in. Her telephone in the compassion sector underscores how gentle and caring she intends to be when either declining to represent or reviewing manuscripts submitted by writers. All interactions are dispatched by phone; therefore, it is the tool through which she conveys genuine concern for and sensitivity to others. No matter how concerned and genuine your feelings are, a positive potency is increased when symbolically displayed in the compassion area.

Computer

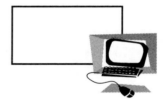

- Positive—You possess a fierce sense of loyalty, a reverent commitment to work, and can be depended on to finish a task appropriately.

Computer in the compassion area

- Challenging—Because of your intense focus on ideas and tasks, your ability to understand co-workers is compromised.

Telephone

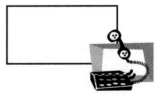

- Positive—If work depends on communication with outside sources, positioning a telephone in this section indicates a real feeling for and concern about those with whom you communicate.

Telephone in the compassion area

- Challenging—You would rather be dealing with anyone else but co-workers at the office.

Printer

- Positive—You want your output to be as pristine and perfect as possible and risk overlooking other forms of communication as valid.

Printer in the compassion area

- Challenging—Others may feel as if you are not sufficiently interested in anything about them other than their productivity.

Fax Machine

- Positive—You take a great deal of responsibility for making sure that your company is perceived correctly by the general public or your specific customers.

Fax machine in the compassion area

- Challenging—You may be focusing on access to customers and ignoring your colleagues. By not considering co-workers' valuable input, you may feel alone and under a great deal of pressure. Listen to others and lighten your load.

Picture of Loved Ones

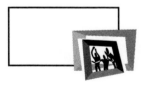

- Positive—Family is your central focus, and all decisions are based on what is best for them, not necessarily what you desire personally.

Picture of loved ones in the compassion area

- Challenging—What is happening in your personal life affects your performance at work. Colleagues experience you as detached.

Rolodex

- Positive—Quick to respond, seek assistance, or network, you have excellent promotional skills.
- Challenging—You may not seek outside support for talents that may already exist within

Rolodex in the compassion area

your company. If you work alone, you may not trust yourself to make appropriate decisions or are unable to perform without assistance or affirmation.

Pens and Pencils

- Positive—Others feel you take what they say seriously.
- Challenging—Colleagues may be extraordinarily careful expressing themselves in your presence because of the concern that you will pull apart and dissect whatever they say.

Pens and pencils in the compassion area

Pads of Paper

- Positive—Often annoyed by those who talk too much rather than engage in the process of completing tasks, you dislike to be interrupted. It is likely that you produce a great deal during the workday.

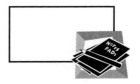

Pads of paper in the compassion area

- Challenging—Knowing that you prefer to see ideas articulated in a memo or other form of written communication, others avoid verbally discussing ideas with you. For that reason you may feel left out of office camaraderie.

"In" Boxes with Work or Just Piles of Work Papers

- Positive—Always ready to accept more than a share of a workload, your dependability is treasured by co-workers.

"In" boxes in the compassion area

- Challenging—You feel the burdensome weight of the company rests firmly on your shoulders and you relentlessly and seriously pursue responsibilities.

Desk Lamp

- Positive—Truthfulness and honesty are the only ways you handle situations. When it comes to understanding how to deal sensitively with others, you are a master and a model to emulate.

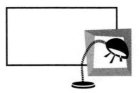

Desk lamp in the compassion area

- Challenging—You are far too critical of others and may seek to assign blame elsewhere prior to examining your own accountability.

Empty Space

- Positive—With the ability to listen without judging, you are sought out when others need a sounding board on which to test ideas or discuss problems.

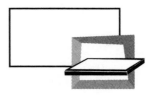

Empty space in the compassion area

- Challenging—Others may feel as if they have to stand on their heads to get you to make a decision or give an opinion.

Cluttered Space

- Positive—Accepting of all situations, you tend to make time to listen to whomever needs you.
- Challenging—Others may feel timid about approaching you and asking for help. This may hinder your ability to evaluate input clearly or be seen as a team player.

Clutter in the compassion area

Items to Place in the Compassion Area

Fire—to ignite your ability to empathize: red candle or red bowl for paperclips

Earth—to provide a safe haven for people to express themselves: dark wood box

Metal—to help those who seek your counsel and to be able to help them articulate their ideas or feelings: chrome or silver pen

Water—to promote intimacy and sharing of confidences: tissues in a floral or undulating patterned container

Wood—to enhance others' ability to stop engaging in pettiness: striped pencil container

Self

Where you sit at a desk is the area of self. Your source of power is usually positioned there. Why would a typist put a telephone close by or an accountant a Rolodex? We tend to have close at hand those items that help us express ourselves most exquisitely.

Self area—where the desk chair is typically positioned

Just as a person is best served throughout life by developing avenues that will augment natural proclivities, objects that help us achieve the highest and best work should be placed in the self area.

> The vehicle through which you express your premium talent sits in the self area.

If your work is multitasked, it is better to keep this area empty. If the item placed in the self area is one in which you rely on greatly to achieve results, then the care given to that item parallels your self-esteem.

My laptop sits squarely in front of me during those periods when I am writing a book. After completing each book, I move the computer to another desktop location to facilitate focusing on other tasks normally relegated to the back burner during a book writing process.

In general, the most comfortable arena through which you make use of your talents is best positioned close at hand, yet many of the desktop dozen would rarely be placed permanently in the self position. For that reason, printer, desk lamp, "in" boxes, Rolodex, picture of loved ones, and fax machine are eliminated from the following list.

Computer

- Positive—You are consistent and dependable. The work accomplished on the computer reflects your best efforts.
- Challenging—Like an ostrich with its head in the sand, you sometimes can't see the big picture because of your intense focus on details.

Computer in the self area

Telephone

- Positive—Never shirking responsibilities, you are ready to reach out and connect with those who are important in your work.
- Challenging—You may tend to rely on outside sources rather than the talents close by.

Telephone in the self area

Pens and Pencils

- Positive—You are receptive to new ideas, yours or others.
- Challenging—Others might be hesitant to run ideas by you since you tend to remember those that didn't work more than those that did.

Pens and pencils in the self area

Pads of Paper

- Positive—Overflowing with
  enthusiasm and ideas, your
  mind is never turned off
  from thinking about how to
  improve, augment, and
  enhance business success.

*Pads of paper in the
self area*

- Challenging—You may not
  be able to really listen to others, or you may give
  only the appearance of focusing on verbal
  communication.

Empty Space

- Positive—Having a clear
  mind to discern the best
  way to approach a project,
  you are sensitive to the
  needs of the moment.

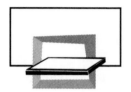

Empty space in the self area

- Challenging—You may be
  uncomfortable with working
  quietly and independently.

Cluttered Space

- Positive—You are brimming
  with too many ideas and
  actions.

Clutter in the self area

- Challenging—Clutter in the
  self position exposes a
  person who has difficulty
  coping with a demanding
  workload. Many times your good ideas get lost or
  forgotten because of the clutter.

Items to Place in the Self Area

Fire—to assist with fulfilling your potential: red leather blotter

Earth—to boost confidence in your own ability: square handmade paper surface

Metal—to strengthen the ability to call on inner resolve: silver- or gold-cover notebook

Water—to keep a balanced focus on your emotional impact: black accessories

Wood—to promote acceptance of change: mint or pine oil dropped on desktop or in a diffuser

Wisdom

The area in a room most likely to be underutilized is the wisdom area. Directly to the left of a room's threshold is an area likely to be ignored. When entering a room, a person tends to glance to the right and then proceed to a prede-

Wisdom area—to the left of where you sit

termined destination. Unless there is an architectural reason to look to the left, most of us tend to enter a space quickly, glance straight ahead toward the back wall, and then rotate toward

How you integrate the benefits of life's formal and informal learning is indicated by what you place in the wisdom area.

the right. This natural pattern precludes the likelihood that the area to the left of the threshold will be noticed.

Interaction with a desktop is different. We have more connection with and have access to the immediate left side. Therefore, the wisdom position on the desk has a slightly different meaning than it does in a room.

Unless a person is left-handed, greater effort is used to place papers or look at objects on the left side. Thus what is placed on the desktop to the left of where you sit is likely to represent more disagreeable chores or urgent tasks.

The least favorite task in my world is to call media people to procure publicity, yet by placing my marketing phone in the wisdom area I am prodded to notice this annoying task. If a pile of urgent work is lying to your left, you are agonizing over it and probably feel ecstatic when it is whittled down. Those placing the to-do pile to the left feel less able to control their workload and have a harder time saying no to new projects.

Consider what you have placed directly to the left of your desk chair, for it represents what you perceive as challenges. The good news is that by placing those arduous tasks close at hand you communicate that you are squarely facing responsibilities, not sequestering them out of sight or neglecting to complete them.

Computer

- Positive—What is produced on this piece of office equipment represents a great deal of value to the company.
- Challenging—Probably not your favorite office tool, you may be avoiding using this equipment more than is advisable.

Computer in the wisdom area

Telephone

- Positive—You have cultivated an ability to communicate because you know that what you accomplish with this instrument is critical to a job's success.

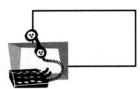

Telephone in the wisdom area

- Challenging—Unless you are deaf in your right ear, positioning the phone on this side usually means that having successful interactions on the telephone feels like a formidable task.

Printer

- Positive—With a healthy respect for deadlines, you are extremely concerned that your output is refined and polished and you have a tenacious focus to accomplish this.

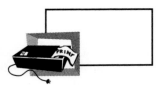

Printer in the wisdom area

- Challenging—You may feel insecure about verbally communicating ideas and need to substantiate them via the written word.

Fax Machine

- Positive—You are likely to be a great spokesperson for your company. You are on top of public relations and are aware of consumer satisfaction.

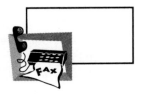

Fax machine in the wisdom area

- Challenging—You might be focusing more on consumer

relations than on interoffice functioning, which could be a disservice to overall job satisfaction and reduce chances of advancement.

Picture of Loved Ones

Picture of loved ones in the wisdom area

- Positive—A deep and abiding sense of family comforts and sustains your life.
- Challenging—You may be spending too much energy focusing on your personal life, which reduces optimum functioning; hence you may find sustaining employment difficult.

Rolodex

Rolodex in the wisdom area

- Positive—Wisely safeguarding all connections, you are a master at networking and reap its rewards.
- Challenging—Feeling insecure about accomplishing diverse tasks, you are likely to trust others' opinions before your own.

Pens and Pencils

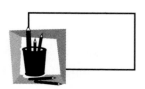

Pens and pencils in the wisdom area

- Positive—Not likely to make rash decisions, you tend to think about things longer than most.
- Challenging—You often overlook your own ideas in favor of those generated by others.

Pads of Paper

- Positive—People can depend on you to keep your word and remember what has transpired.

Pads of paper in the wisdom area

- Challenging—Rigid and uncomfortable with change, you do not give new ideas or procedures the appropriate time to flourish.

"In" Boxes with Work or Just Piles of Work Papers

- Positive—Just like a pad and pencil next to your bed is a must for those with ideas that flourish just before or during sleep, keeping paper ready in the wisdom position indicates an active and fertile mind.

"In" boxes in the wisdom area

- Challenging—No one takes his or her responsibility more seriously than you do. While this is generally an asset, it produces a great deal of strain and causes you to feel encumbered.

Desk Lamp

- Positive—You get to the heart of a matter quickly and are not blinded by smoke screens released to obscure truth.

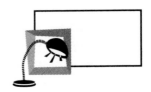

Desk lamp in the wisdom area

- Challenging—Fearing mistakes, you scrutinize

work endlessly, which gives rise to tension. You may experience more than your share of head- or neck aches.

Empty Space

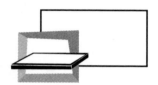

Empty space in the wisdom area

- Positive—Likely to give others a chance to be heard, you are a good listener.
- Challenging—Your need to be perceived as an authority adds personal pressure, for you rarely ask for help.

Cluttered Space

Clutter in the wisdom area

- Positive—Like a sponge, you effectively soak up information and pride yourself on being aware of the cutting-edge information in your industry.
- Challenging—Overwhelmed by the workload, your adrenals are probably working overtime, which can cause frequent illness or fitful worry.

Items to Place in the Wisdom Area

Fire—to train yourself to accept outside assistance: book of quotes

Earth—to give you a deep sense of security about trusting your instincts: a cherished or childhood dictionary or an award statue

Metal—to aid in articulating ideas: a clear marble, small crystal, or reduced-by-75-percent replica of an award or diploma

Water—to dispel self-doubt and promote confidence: a thesaurus

Wood—to inspire creativity and generate ideas: book of puzzles or Rubik's Cube

COMMUNITY

Humans are not solitary creatures. Yet in adult life we spend most of the workday alone or working independently. By surrounding ourselves with cherished supports and representations or symbols of others who have shaped our lives, we can make our environment an enduring support system.

Community area—mid-left-hand side of desk

Every classroom, association, and job, when appropriate, prepares us to leap to the next level. This is not always comfortable

> The lifetime supports that have contributed to shaping you are best honored in the community area.

or easy, yet it is necessary. Those who are lucky enough to be in a position where learning is offered have the opportunity to become closer to their ideal self. Situated on the mid-left side of a desk, sandwiched between our self-power and wisdom, is the realm of community. It can be likened to the instrumentation accompanying a vocalist. While it can never be substituted for the vocal talents of the singer, it can make the song richer and deeper and provide a fuller meaning to listeners.

Computer

- Positive—You are able to draw on myriad personal resources. Feeling loved is central to your life.
- Challenging—You are apt to rely on others more than yourself.

Computer in the community area

Telephone

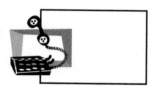

- Positive—Apt to wisely seek others' counsel, you have the talent to be a spokesperson for your company's image, policies, or ideas.
- Challenging—You tend to jump the gun in telling the public or competitors of plans.

Telephone in the community area

Printer

- Positive—You feel directly responsible for bridging the gap between company policy and public awareness.
- Challenging—You may depend on what others tell you to do rather than your own intuition.

Printer in the community area

Fax Machine

- Positive—Networking is a strength. You are always ready to be a spokesperson for your company's ideas.
- Challenging—You may be relying on the reactions of others too much or hope that others will help miraculously send information needed.

Fax machine in the community area

Picture of Loved Ones

- Positive—You are deeply aware of how your destiny has been shaped.
- Challenging—You struggle to release detrimental life events to be in harmony with your inner self.

Picture of loved ones in the community area

Rolodex

- Positive—Not likely to let anyone slip through the cracks, you are likely to have a huge source of contacts to call on.
- Challenging—Not comfortable with changing employment, you might stay at an unsuitable job for too long.

Rolodex in the community area

Pens and Pencils

- Positive—Writing notes or E-mail to friends is a great source of pleasure for you. Your holiday card list is generally long and filled with people connected to you throughout all stages of your life.

Pens and pencils in the community area

- Challenging—You might rely on standard business practices rather than accept the challenge to innovate new ones.

Pads of Paper

- Positive—A rich reservoir of lifetime supports gives you an edge when seeking a variety of ways to approach a problem.

Pads of paper in the community area

- Challenging—Feeling shortchanged in childhood advantages, you have to cope with feelings of jealousy and may blame others too frequently.

"In" Boxes with Work or Just Piles of Work Papers

- Positive—You have a secure feeling that no matter what the workload is you will be able to accomplish it with distinction.

"In" boxes in the community area

- Challenging—You may feel as if others manipulate your life and find a penetrating melancholy diffused in your daily experience.

Desk Lamp

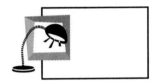

Desk lamp in the community area

- Positive—Clearly self-preserving, you are able to take as good care of yourself as those others who did in your past.
- Challenging—Needing to be the center of attention, you often overlook the value of others in the past and the benefits you have derived from them.

Empty Space

Empty space in the community area

- Positive—If the past was filled with difficult experiences, an empty space in the community position indicates that you have moved beyond them. If your past was generally productive and supportive, having empty space in this area indicates your willingness to embrace new ways and friends.
- Challenging—Feeling as if you are alone in the world and have no one to depend on makes the path on which you tread lonely and keeps you alert for treachery.

Cluttered Space

- Positive—You have
  successfully culled only
  the positive from the past
  and have rendered the
  damaging innocuous.

*Clutter in the
community area*

- Challenging—You haven't
  a clue about how to
  resolve those things in your past that
  block today's successes.

Items to Place in the Community Area

Fire—to spark the intention to resolve obstacles
stemming from past experiences: red picture frame

Earth—to help you cherish the best from a lifetime of
experiences: a wooden desktop toy

Metal—to reduce the likelihood that the past will
negatively impact today: a calendar with gold or
silver lettering

Water—to help uncover the supports existing in your
workplace: glass vase with water and a vine or a
small recirculating fountain

Wood—to be steeled with resolve to alter past
negative influences: aged green copper box or pen-
carrying case

HEALTH

Being in optimum health in the workplace relates to utilizing
your innate aptitudes in a way that is deeply satisfying. Since
a great deal of adult life is spent engaged in job-related activ-

ities, compromising emotional contentment for possible future rewards offers no benefit. Health in the workplace implies reaching equilibrium, a state in which we are stimulated to engage in activities but feeling relaxed while

Health area—middle of desk

doing so. We should reach the point of being able to address our ambitions without compromising mental and physical health.

When pursuing tasks that are aligned strategically to your inner self, you should have no feelings of stress. When you are engaged in something you love, time is suspended. Only when you forsake your natural assets are you unable to grapple with problems and strategize successfully. Health therefore is the ability to be engaged in work that for the most part is aligned with your natural talents.

Some of the desktop dozen are not typically positioned in the center of the desk; therefore, some of the items have been eliminated just as they were in the self area. Even though the choices are limited, know that what is typically positioned there is a key to discovering if you are engaged in the right work. When a workplace does not fulfill a core part of who you are, pressure can build over time, causing pessimism, exhaustion, frustration, and depression.

What is placed in the health area on a desktop reveals if you are likely to use or dissipate talents, energy, and time.

Computer

- Positive—You feel satisfied and gratified by your accomplishments at work.
- Challenging—Like a guillotine ready to drop, your workload looms ominously over each day, depleting your confidence and energy.

Computer in the health area

Telephone

- Positive—Your personality and mental acumen have no barriers in being communicated through this equipment.
- Challenging—Your output on this machine determines your status and success at work, and you feel pressure to continuously improve and to communicate effectively.

Telephone in the health area

Rolodex

- Positive—Keeping a Rolodex or any other telephone list in the health area communicates gratitude for the wealth of resources offered by those recorded there.
- Challenging—You may feel as if you are drowning in a sea of responsibility to others and are unable to find a way to lighten your load.

Rolodex in the health area

Pens and Pencils

- Positive—You are ready to tackle additional tasks. Others come to you when a volunteer or recruit is needed.
- Challenging—You may sometimes jump the gun and respond too quickly before thinking clearly about a situation or an idea.

Pens and pencils in the health area

Pads of Paper

- Positive—You are likely to feel confident about ideas and unafraid to seek new venues or try unusual solutions.
- Challenging—You are likely to fritter away time with redundancies. You might be a secret computer hearts or solitaire player.

Pads of paper in the health area

"In" Boxes with Work or Just Piles of Work Papers

- Positive—You can be relied on not to let a task slip away unattended and assume the lion's share of responsibility for completing tasks.
- Challenging—You may feel so pressured from work that functioning at optimum is impaired.

"In" boxes in the health area

Empty Space

- Positive—You are able to function clearly and effectively even when there is a tremendous workload.
- Challenging—You may be working at a position that demands more than you feel capable of doing and therefore may delegate too quickly those responsibilities that are not in your comfort zone.

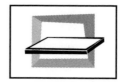

Empty space in the health area

Cluttered Space

- Positive—Since exploring and learning thrills you, it is sometimes impossible to stop the process to do housekeeping.
- Challenging—You wish to pare down self-imposed challenges and use clutter to obstruct productivity.

Clutter in the health area

Nothing is accidental. The selection of common objects on a desk or work surface either facilitates a process or exposes the liabilities that hinder success. Evaluating the potential message reveals a picture that will expose why you function the way you do. By moving desktop items to locations that facilitate functioning at optimum, you become your own coach and help facilitate the achievement of your goals.

The layouts in Appendix A represent a generic configuration for some occupations. This gives you an idea of a generic but positive layout. Remember, even if you hold one of these positions, you are still unique and need to distinguish your desktop to fit you specifically.

By changing desktop elements to positions that can support improved behavior, reactions, or methodologies, we can nudge ourselves toward our goals with less stress and angst. Only by stepping outside of our customary routines can we activate the potential to make quantum leaps.

11

A Box of My Own

The Cubicle

N o matter how small the space you control, it can be enhanced to suit your needs. When you need to feel calm, more relaxed, energized, or alert, fear not. There are ways to improve the surrounding space, no matter how small.

Cubicle Essentials

If you have ever moved into a new home and felt the space was larger when the furnishings were in place, you have encountered the phenomenon of proportion. To make a small space feel larger, put small objects in it.

When an article is placed in empty space, it defines the amount of space, as well as providing a focus for the eye. Adding a small mat or rug to the floor at the threshold of the cubicle makes the rest of the cubicle seem larger. Moreover, by having a threshold defined you have furnished a place for common rules of etiquette to be followed. When strangers or friends come to your home unexpectedly, they expect that you, the owner of the space, will open the door and invite them in. It is polite to be invited into someone's personal space at either the exterior or interior threshold. A small mat by the threshold will encourage this expectation, and you will find that others do not intrude upon your space without an invitation to enter.

Paintings, calendars, and paper hung on the wall should be large enough to view when entering the cubicle, and small enough to see in their entirety when seated. Many people hang very small things on their cubicle walls that can only be seen clearly when seated. When the eye converges on these small spaces it is primed to seek other similarly scaled objects; hence the focus becomes of the minutia. By encouraging focus on seated-level objects, the space feels smaller.

Minimize reflective surfaces. Just as using a cell phone in an automobile can be potentially hazardous because the unnaturally high electro and magnetic frequencies can't escape the car's metal frame, reflective surfaces in a confined work space can be hazardous to your health. In general, reflective surfaces bombard you with light, which forces attention to detail. This is not a negative condition if there are relief surfaces on which the eye can remain motionless. Too many reflective surfaces in a space the size of a cubicle can add to a feeling of tenseness and excitability over time.

Hang or place a mid- to deep-colored object across from the most frequently used piece of office equipment, which is typically the computer. Select a color (or colors) that promotes what you need (refer to Chapter 12, which includes detailed lists of colors and what they add emotionally), but in general use:

- Rose to mid-red when it is important to be empathetic and forceful
- Beige to cocoa when you need to emphasize a feeling of stability and calmness
- Gray, mustard, or mat copper when you want to sharpen your mental acuity and be able to conceive alternatives

- Charcoal or medium blue to promote self-sufficiency and assuredness of reaching a goal
- Green to teal when it is important to infuse new ideas or be able to adjust to shifting parameters

The Seven Deadly Cubicle Sins and How to Cure Them

The following situations may sound familiar. Here's how you can remedy them.

1. A pathway adjacent to a cubicle gives colleagues an unimpeded view inside the work space as they pass by.

Cure

Position a tall plant on the floor between you and office traffic. Although you won't be completely concealed, the sight lines between you and others will be blurred. It takes only the slightest veiling to ensure that you feel shielded.

2. Hearing an unending mechanical noise originating from an elevator, heating systems, air ducts, or other machinery can be a maddening irritant in a workplace. I remember spending summers working in a factory where heavy machinery pounded out metal shapes. These sounds were so familiar that I thought they did not interrupt or influence my output until the day of an electricity outage. I was struck by the serenity of silence and how much easier it was to concentrate and produce results. Whether we are aware of it or not, when noises are neither natural nor positive in association, our minds have to work in overdrive to screen them out.

Cure

Fight fire with fire and set up a pleasant sound–producing alternative in your work area. Be sure that it is both inoffensive and nonintrusive to others yet soothing to you. Music from clocks, radios, or chimes can counteract machine noise. One of my clients who had a great deal of trouble concentrating brought a metronome to work and found its marking of time as soothing as listening to a heartbeat.

3. White or black partitions surrounding a cubicle. Staring day after day at a highly reflective white surface, which exaggerates mental processes, or a black one, which appears to be a hole and therefore dissipates the security of a surrounding edge, does not inspire a feeling of contentment. As discussed earlier, every color inspires feelings, and it is vital that you have the option to insert in your cubicle colors that will both refresh and energize the space for you.

Cure

Keep a stack of colored paper or a few selections of pictures with different color fields ready to push-pin into the wall at eye level with your seated position. For example, a field of daffodils cut from a gardening catalog is my vision for clarity and illumination, which is inspired by the color yellow. If a push pin cannot be pounded into a partition, use double-sided tape or restickable adhesive. Selection of colors depends on needs:

Red to energize
Blue to relax
Green to generate ideas
Yellow to clarify
Tan or brown for stability
Black to visualize a goal
White to generate mental activity

4. No depth view. Biological adaptation is a wondrous achievement when you consider how one feature of an organism compensates for the deficiency of another and thereby advances a species' survival options. Consider the prowess of adaptation of the human being, which has neither lethal teeth nor claws and moves at a snail's pace compared to other primates. One adaptation, which has accorded survival, is farsightedness. Human beings see farther into the distance than many other species, making it possible to see danger coming before it is within striking zone. One detriment of a cubicle is that it does not allow our eyes to switch between close up and far away. Many readers of this book may have discovered their rapidly declining eyesight after working at a computer. Not being able to change from looking close up to far away accounts for much of the diminishing visual acuity.

Cure

Hang a picture with a vanishing point in view behind your computer. A scene with a pathway leading into a markedly three-dimensional scene with near and far objects is the kind of picture to select. If hanging a picture is not an option, position a refracting object nearby to attract the eye's attention to alternate from close up to a distance.

Picture with a vanishing point hung behind computer

5. Is there a high pile blocking a view to your desk?
Objects that hinder a view to the heart of a space (your desk
is most likely the heart of your work area) are considered *sha
chi*. In this case, *sha chi* simply means it is negative to have any
physical condition that obstructs, minimizes, or reduces your
access to an important area. File cabinets piled with stuff near
the threshold of a cubicle often prevent you from fully sur-
veying a work surface. A parallel in a home would be a hutch
obstructing part of your formal dining table or a dresser cutting one side of your bed from view when entering these rooms.

Cure

If rearranging the obstructing piece of equipment is out of the
question, position a mirror on an observable wall that reflects
the entire surface of your desk.

**6. Are there any piles of material or a computer tower
higher than the top of your head when seated?** If you grew
up with older siblings you know the feeling of being too small.
Having objects looming over you creates *sha chi*. Feeling diminished can influence your capacity to excel. The more stuff that
is piled on top of a desk, the greater your frustration that you
will never finish or accomplish enough.

Cure

Move the computer tower off the desk. In this case the floor
adjacent to the desk is appropriate. Consider which desktop
items are used daily and which are not. Tape holders, tissue
boxes, reference books, and samples are best kept inside drawers or on shelves close by. There should be nothing taller than
you at a desk.

A cardinal rule: If you don't use it daily, take it
off the desk.

7. Are edges of file cabinets, tables, or tabletop equipment facing you when you work? Have you ever noticed how jarring it can be when something comes into your peripheral field of vision? Facing edges of objects is *sha chi*. A glimpse of something partial is more unnerving than viewing the whole object because it takes more piecing together in one's brain to fill in the missing content. Hence, a moment of uncertainty is created that can cause apprehension. In confined spaces, having a

Sha chi is the negative condition created by large or pointed objects seemingly aimed in your direction.

partial view of an object is like peripheral information and distracts concentration.

Cure

Place a vase filled with trailing vines covering the edge, a lamp with a round base, or a tri-fold screen to camouflage edges of equipment or furniture. Chunky, earthy, cylindrical shapes will avert attention to an edge when placed at eye level.

PERSONALIZING A SPACE

Each and every work space should reflect its proprietor's uniqueness and be identifiable as such the moment it is entered. Aside from the commonplace selections such as photographs, desk accessories, or a favored pen, icons displayed need to be connected to other segments of life. A single piece from a home collection is one good way to tie parts of life together. I collect dragons, and the clock hung across from my desk contains this symbol. Julie Kroll has personalized her computer's screen saver with scenes from Chicago, her hometown. An afghan knitted by a favorite aunt draped over the back of a desk chair, a child's ceramic artwork, a piece of nautical equipment from your sailboat, or a golf trophy would be a personal symbol that can transform an impersonal space. If who you are is not immediately apparent, you are not fleshing out a picture of your full self at work and may discover that others do not appreciate the richness of your personhood.

Image a cubicle as a womb protecting you from harm. It can alter the way you feel about your work space. In the same way it feels comforting to read a book by a roaring fire or lie on a bed of soft grass, a cubicle can be beneficial if fashioned in a way that protects, connects, and projects your personality.

12

OWNWORK/HOMEWORK

The Joys and Perils of Working at Home

Many while away hours dreaming of a day when the bedroom and boardroom will be under one roof. With technology advancing faster than a speeding bullet, there is no reason why many can't carve out a work niche at home. However, before making the leap, determine whether the romance of convenience can outweigh the cold air of solitude. Freedom of choice may be outweighed by the insecurity of an irregular paycheck. There are considerations to ponder prior to trading the nine-to-five clock for the five-to-nine one.

TIME

Clocks don't exist when you work at home. The time is always now. While you may be able to paddle to the computer with less than a one-minute commute, you'll find it equally hard to tear yourself away at night and shuffle off to sleep.

Even if a business or service can function only between business hours, there is a great deal of work that can be accomplished before or after. One of the downsides to working at home is that stopping work can be harder than beginning to work. Just like a frightening scene in an old science fiction movie, work can be as consuming as an escaped fungus from a distant planet. What starts out looking innocuous grows into an unwieldy mass that sucks up all life it encounters. Social life, hobbies, and quality time with family can be the victim of its swelling mass. It may be necessary to work long hours, but it is not necessary to have no hours.

Strategies for Limiting Time in the Office

Select your own business hours. Don't be concerned if they are 6:00 A.M. to 4:00 P.M. or 10:00 A.M. to 8:00 P.M. The reason to work at home aside from convenience is to be able to use a day in a way more naturally suited to you. Morning people can be rather useless after 3:00 P.M.; therefore adjusting a schedule to fit your own rhythms can make you be more efficient and productive. My home office schedule begins at 5:00 A.M. and drops dead at 3:00 P.M.

Splitting the day is another way to fit in activities that you enjoy. The only way I can extend my productive workday is to take a short nap midday. If I am able to rest, I can work effectively until early evening.

Many of us have discovered that placing a telephone call between noon and 2:00 P.M. is mostly unproductive. Working at home affords you the opportunity to engage in a personal activity, other than eating, during those hours. A health club's midday class, a walk or jog, or shopping can be exhilarating and rejuvenate your enthusiasm for work. Productivity is not always linked to the amount of time spent at a job as much as to the quality of alertness and the ability to be in the flow.

Most important, set specific daily goals to alleviate the feeling that work is never done. Divide activities that make sense into time slots during the day. For example, if your creative juices overflow only during morning's early hours, be sure to engage only in creative activities during those hours. Late morning might be a time to catch up on all your least favorite work chores, whose accomplishment is the reward of lunch or a midday activity. Afternoons may be filled with connecting and communicating, with phone calls or correspondence. By outlining standard objectives, you will feel justified in leaving the office at day's end.

Choose a timepiece that marks the passage of time with a sound to help you adhere to a schedule. For example, a cuckoo clock with a large penetrating hourly sound becomes like an hourly metronome, giving a pulse beat to the day's activities.

A computer's alarm clock can alert you to the schedule for completion of certain goals. Setting a reasonable limit for certain activities and knowing when the time is over helps you stay on track and keep abreast of productivity.

Consider placing an hourglass on your desk to aid telephone awareness. A celebrated public relations person who has a client list that makes the nighttime sky look dull told me that she keeps an egg timer near the phone to limit her pitches. After

Desirable Characteristics of a Home Work Space Location

- Access to a bathroom without having to go to another part of the house
- A door leading outside
- No home phone
- Clock, coffee or tea maker
- Access to business machinery such as printer, fax, copy machine, drawing board, etc.
- Access to daily supplies, such as papers, brochures, stamps, boxes, and pens

years in the business, she knows that a person's attention span can tolerate only three minutes. If you have ever listened to a long-winded message on an answering machine and become impatient with the caller's ramblings, you can see how limiting the communication time can be in your own best interest. Brevity can be an ally when casting out bait to potential customers/clients.

Which Room to Pick

Even though the beginnings of home businesses are often humble, do not start in a preexisting desk location. The desk was located in that position for an entirely different set of needs from those that exist for a business. Imagine opening a retail store and using the layout of the former tenant. The thought would never cross your mind. But using a desk located in a corner of a bedroom or choosing a room simply because it is available is equally preposterous.

It is important to provide a buffer between work and home. Passing a work area during times better served by relaxing is another pitfall of working at home. No matter which room or area you select, by following these simple feng shui suggestions you can widen the space between work and home. Remember that all work and no play wears down creative processes. Consider these suggestions to buffer any work space from the distractions of home.

Buffering a Work Space from Home Space

1. Select a room that is contained. I am amazed by how often people locate integral parts of their office supplies outside their office space. Strange as it may sound, it took me a long time to reverse a lifetime habit of keeping stamps in the

kitchen. Your work flow will be unrestrained if all the pieces necessary to your work process are close by.

2. Hang a doorknocker or drape a bell over the room's doorknob. Install a lock on the door. This will telegraph a message that it is inappropriate to barge in without asking permission.

3. Shield the space from disturbing noises.

- Hang an area rug on the wall to buffer sound from other rooms.
- Place a water feature close to the work area (white noise screens out distracting chatter, street noises, or other sounds that divert focus).

4. Use a fragrance not used elsewhere in a home. The scent need only be disseminated for less than fifteen minutes to convey a sense of place to the work space. Here are some suggestions for fragrances that can add to productivity and contentment during those time frames.

Morning—sage, frankincense, laurel, rosemary
After lunch—peppermint, mint, tea tree, clary sage, eucalyptus
Late afternoon—lime or grapefruit, yarrow, bergamot, chamomile

5. Remove any carpeting from the pathway approaching the office area. This will allow you to hear approaching footsteps, which will give you more time to prepare for an interruption.

6. Place a screen or plant as a second threshold inside the office door to camouflage the work area from sight. This will also help you borrow time before an interruption.

7. Place the phone and fax on mute once you've left your office for the day. This separates personal time from professional life.

Even if you have a spare bedroom or a basement that could lend itself to work, be sure you consider all the options before choosing a location. A room presently used for other activities may turn out to be a better choice. The following sections describe possible locations, explain why you might want to move your office there, and tell how to handle the activities that were previously carried out there.

Main Bedroom

In many newer homes the main or master bedroom is separated from the others, situated on the other side of the house or divided by a hallway or bathroom. Situating a work space in that area has some distinct advantages:

- It insulates the work areas from home activities and may help you resist the siren call of work after hours.
- Many master bedrooms also have two outer walls, which cocoon the work area further.
- Typically a main bedroom is large enough to accommodate an extra chair, which will make a visitor, child, or mate feel welcomed in your office.
- Many main bedrooms have a private bathroom, which not only lends an air of self-sufficiency but also precludes the need to wander away from the work area. It is easier to be distracted from work and interested in home activities when you have to leave the work area.

If you decide to make the main bedroom an office, be sure that everything you want in a master bedroom can be accommodated elsewhere in the home. A smaller bedroom, for example, may not have enough room for the intimate conversation grouping that you now have. Don't sacrifice that feature; relocate it to another room.

Basement

If the only place to accommodate a work space is down under, it is imperative to remember to add a complete complement of sensory experiences. A work space without connection to the outdoors needs the following:

Air Movement

A fan aimed at a plant (silk is fine) replicates what it feels like to be outside.

Scent

Tie a scent-doused ribbon on a fan's protective cover over the blade and let the breeze disseminate its fragrance. Have two or three different ribbons to use during the course of a day or week:

- If your basement is damp—rosemary or laurel
- If your basement is cool—neroli or spikenard
- If your basement is hot—sandalwood, fennel, or lemon
- If you feel isolated when working there—cedarwood, geranium rose, or ginger

Pattern

When there is not a tapestry of colors or natural movement of shadows in a space, it is imperative to replicate them by adjusting patterns. Pick out a texture with a nonpredictable repeat pattern. For example, checkers would generally not be good, but undulating stripes of varying thicknesses would.

*Predictable patterns are not good for basement
offices, but ones that vary are.*

Color

Under no circumstances should you select a monochromatic
scheme. Colors in the middle to light range of saturation are
best. Deep colors or fully saturated colors align us to our physical selves and may be distracting or counterproductive in a
basement work space unless used sparingly as accents. Consider
what emotional assistance is needed at work and choose a color
that provides it:

- Corn-kernel yellow if encouragement and relief from
  feeling burdened is needed
- Periwinkle blue if you tend to worry about others'
  opinions
- Sage or leaf green if you are stuck in a rut and need
  to risk making changes or find the uncommon
  solution
- Beige or whites to stimulate the flow of ideas
- Red to sustain a high level of activity
- Bright orange to promote proactive communication

Use fire colors such as oranges and reds only as accents.
Since the basement relates to the earth element, adding too much
fire can make it feel volatile, like a volcano waiting to erupt.

Attic

Attics can be ideal for those who need to feel detached from home activities to be fruitful. An attic may have a steeply pitched ceiling, which makes that room a fire element, inspiring and energizing. Since many attics have unusual windows, this room will feel different from others and generate a fresh perspective.

If daydreaming gets out of hand in this room, ground your work area with a brown- or red-toned area rug. Here are some other ideas for turning an attic room into a successful work space.

Colors

If there is an abundance of light or a glare from windows, choose middle-range to deep colors.

- Rhododendron green can create a feeling of being in the commanding catbird position and can spawn a fuller, more detached perspective on situations.
- The blue of a clear or cloudless sky helps retrieve ideas lodged in the mind's deepest recesses.
- Choose only muted deep reds and oranges for attic decor. When colors are too bold, an attic can become too energizing, making getting down to work hard. If you are a parent, you may have noticed that children are much more rambunctious when surrounded by bright reds in combination with other primary colors.

Sound

An attic needs an ambient sound. Music with a nonspecific or nonrepetitive melody is ideal. If you cannot work with music in a work space, try a clock with a pendulum, a water feature with water splashing randomly onto a surface, or a fan directed at a plant with enough air movement to cause the leaves to rustle.

Air Movement

Whenever possible, crack a window or install a ceiling fan.

Scent

A water-element scent can balance an attic's normally dry and warm conditions. Some suggestions are:

- Juniper—can help you tackle work alone
- Red thyme—good for those beginning a business because this scent instills courage and assertiveness.
- Ginger—boosts morale and helps manifest drive to complete unactualized plans.

Texture

Because of the lack of earth element, open-weave or loosely woven textures are more likely to preserve balance when working in an attic. Leathers or tight synthetic weaves will disturb a serene atmosphere.

A Secondary Bedroom or Spare Room

Carefully consider the use of rooms in a home before eliminating a spare bedroom or other room as an office. No need to have a room devoted wholly to guests if the total visiting time is less than one month each year. So often we delegate the use of rooms based on what is perceived as the norm. Consider the need for a formal dining room in a home that has an ample and attractive eat-in kitchen. Is the desire for entertaining formally so ingrained or the amount of time spent entertaining so great that not having a formal room would be a deprivation? An office enclosed with four walls is far better than one located in a corner of a room. Therefore, consider carefully all rooms' uses. If a room is not used daily, perhaps its function should be relegated elsewhere.

Here are some ways to transform a guest room or other seldom used room into a home office.

Entrance

Treat the entrance to this room as if it were an outside threshold:

- Install a lock on the entrance door.
- Place icons that match on the outside of the entrance door.
- Hang a bell, doorknocker, or door harp on the outside of the entrance door or drape a bell over the doorknob.
- Place a welcome mat outside the entrance door.

Treat the entrance door to a home office as if it were an outside threshold.

Color

Paint this room a different color from other rooms in the home. To feel separate and distinct, a home office is best designed with totally different colors from the rest of a home's decor.

- Adobe or salmon to ensure a serene atmosphere
- Green when new ideas need to be generated regularly

- Blue when being in touch with emotions is a benefit
- Light yellow when you have a hard time remaining at work during the day
- White when mental clarity or detachment from emotions is required
- Teal when you are fearful about the future

Texture

Be sure to have a variety of textures to lean or sit on, depending on the time of day or season:

- Spring or midday—pile
- Summer or morning—smooth
- Fall or late afternoon—uneven or highly tactile
- Winter or evening—heated or heat retaining

Scent

Flood a room with fragrances at least three times per day:

- When you arrive each morning—sage, neroli, or grapefruit to inspire and clarify
- At the warmest time of the day—lavender; geranium or rose to soothe from strain
- Late-afternoon energy drain—lime, lemon, or clary sage to boost morale and energy to finish work

A Section of a Room

Don't despair if there is no room to devote exclusively to a business. While this is not ideal, a few tips can help you choose which rooms to select and how to adapt them appropriately:

- Select a room where no other activities take place during the same time as work.

- Have a screen or plant positioned to screen off other areas from your view and you from others who may be using the space at the same time. If a desk faces the kitchen, you may go there to snack more often than if it were out of view. Facing a gathering room may entice you to clean it, or if you see a washer/dryer you may find yourself doing laundry when it would be better to straighten out a file cabinet.

- Be sure the room's furniture is not facing your back. Based on the biological necessity of being aware of what is behind us, furniture positioned in back of a desk's chair can sabotage working. If the location of the office is integrated into a gathering room, make sure that you are not backed by furniture that steals your focus.

- Do not face the room's other functions. Position the desk with a point of view that is unique to this area. If you tend to sit in a chair in that room facing the same direction as the desk chair, you will not really have a distinguishing work or home area.

- Place a different floor cover under the desk. Be sure the floor space under the desk is different from what is underfoot in the rest of the room. Since your feet are generally touching the floor, what you feel underfoot helps distinguish this area from others.

COLOR: THE HOME OFFICE BONUS

If you've ever worked in a space controlled by someone else, you'll appreciate the freedom you have to arrange and decorate your home office. No matter where you've decided to locate your home office, you can take full advantage of color's meaning to further your goals. Inherent in all colors is meaning that is easy to understand if you observe how the colors are used in nature. The miracle of all content in the physical world is that there is a relationship between the physical part and the emotional message. What a color engenders physically becomes its implied message metaphorically. Before you choose to paint the walls in a home office, consider the following.

Base your choice of colors in part on where you are facing and what you are doing. If, for example, one part of your work includes generating new ideas, select a picture, an artifact, a plant, furniture, or a wall color with shades of green. If concentration and focus are required to keep accounts receivable in order, then white or reflective golds, silver, or coppers are ideal. Use color to transmit a message that is in accord with the work you do.

Green

Green is the most misunderstood color. If you associate green with relaxation as in being in a garden, you are mistaken. The green in your mind is incorporated into a panorama of sensorial experiences. In a garden, forest, or just plain outdoors, consider what is really happening. You feel the air as it moves against your skin with its occasional molecules of scent from adjacent vegetation. Whether it is chirping, honking, revving, or scurrying, sound is generally present. You see, hear, feel, and smell, and that's why you feel so good. Green may be the color most often associated with nature or the great outdoors, but in and of itself it means something entirely different.

Green is the color of chlorophyll, which aids growth. Without chlorophyll a plant either dies or is dormant. Green is therefore the color of change, expansion, augmentation, and movement.

Consider the body's use of green as the color of bile, which is aggravated by too much movement. Seasickness or "feeling green in the face" is a perfect example. Looking at a green wall makes you move, augment, and unfold. Green used sparingly for new businesses or when desiring to expand is advantageous.

Use Green When You . . .
- need a kick-start each day
- are opening a new business
- are trying to capture a new market
- are in an expansion mode
- are stuck in a rut
- need to generate innovations

How Green Can Enhance Your Work
- If ideas are the mainstay of your business, use green striped wallpaper or paint a green stripe on the entrance wall.
- If you need to dare or take chances to be successful, place a green area rug under the desk.
- If you want to change the direction of your business, mount a mostly green picture in a prominent position in the office.
- If you have difficulty feeling energetic and active, trim the closets or windows in green.

Red

For me red immediately conjures up three images: a traffic light, a toreador's flashing red cape, and the Coca-Cola logo. Red captures attention. Red is the longest and slowest light wave, and looking at it is similar to staring at a huge, weighty flag being waved by one person, slow but grand.

The thick foliage of a tropical setting generates the most red berries and flowers. In fact in colder climates red is almost nonexistent because there is less need to be obvious to attract attention. Since tropical flowers rely on winged and legged creatures to carry their seed, the red blooms win the services of these emissaries of procreation. A red blossom simply attracts more activity, and more activity means more potential numbers of the species. In cooler areas, where fewer plants are available, the bees or birds will alight on any plant, not just the ones with colors screaming for attention. In a field of many colors, red is most likely to be chosen.

Red is also the color of the vital fluid that sustains human life. Red enlivens and stimulates.

Use Red When You . . .

- need stimulation
- need to be decisive
- want a cheerleader to spur you on
- want to highlight an icon

How Red Can Enhance Your Work

- If you don't want to waste time, buy a red clock.
- If you want to improve sales, mount the sales record on red paper.
- If you want to focus on your written output, place red felt under a computer.
- If you want to be the center of attention when there are visitors, place a painting with red behind where you sit.

Yellow

While red attracts attention, yellow is the color that clearly defines the outline of a shape. Consider the use of a yellow line to mark a division in a road. The shape of the line jumps out clearly, giving drivers distinct parameters. When children are asked to draw a picture of their homes from the outside, invariably they color the sun yellow. Like the color of cells in our eyes, which control clarity or acuity of vision, yellow is normally associated with defining sharpness of vision. Light, clarity, illumination—whether it be vision or ideas—is associated with the color yellow.

A muted yellow, subtler than the bright primary color used for the sun, transmits a feeling of security and groundedness, particularly for those living in cooler climates. Resonating with the earth element, this tone of yellow will help you focus on listening and being the touchstone for communication in a business setting.

Use Yellow When You . . .

- need stability
- want ideas to crystallize
- want others to seek your advice
- need to get through a task that requires repetition
- need to feel optimistic
- need to focus deeply on one project

How Yellow Can Enhance Your Work

- If you want to focus on formulating ideas, write with a yellow pen or pencil.
- If you want to be mindful of spending money, print a sales record on yellow paper.

- If verbal clarification is an important priority for work, place a yellow felt square under the telephone or in your line of sight when communicating.
- If you need uplifting and encouragement, rest your feet on a small area rug with lots of yellow or drape a yellow cloth over the back of a desk chair.

Blue

We turn blue when we are releasing our life force. When shivering with terror, blood drains from our face and extremities. Blue lips or fingers result from being denied life-supporting warmth. Experiments have shown that body temperature and breathing rate actually lower in a room with blue walls, ceiling, and floors.

Blue is a color of separation, suggesting isolation from others or attention to self. But in a positive sense blue exalts individualization, without necessarily isolating people from each other. The rarity of blue in nature, from a blue moon to a blue bloom, underscores this color's message. Turning inward and being in touch with your essential self is a benefit gained by being surrounded by blue.

Clothing manufacturers know that blue is a favored color of American males. Knowing the symbolic meaning of blue, it is not hard to interpret this archetype. American men are encouraged to be self-reliant, self-generating, and more self-centered than American females. Blue became a preferred color precisely because it expressed these qualities.

Use Blue When You . . .

- need empowerment
- feel confident
- need to relax and feel less nervous

- are about to make a presentation or an important phone call
- need focus and concentration

How Blue Can Enhance Your Work

- If you need to release work-distracting thoughts, cover the desk with a blue cloth.
- If confidence needs bolstering, paint the entrance door blue.
- If you need assistance in saying no, purchase a blue phone or hang a predominantly blue picture on the wall facing you when speaking on the telephone.
- If focus on caring for yourself is waning, purchase blue hanging or manila file folders.
- If your office tends to be too hot, hang blue drapes or install blue flooring.

Orange

Mediating, negotiating, and listening skills can be enhanced when surrounded by orange. Orange is the color of fusion and is a natural selection for groups that are, at their core, aligned to a notion of unity. Just as Buddhist monks have chosen saffron robes as their garb, an era that bridges two disparate ways of thinking often uses orange. Designers in the 1960s, for example, brought orange into clothing and furniture.

FedEx was an instant success in part because of its choice of colors. Orange juxtaposed with blue communicates fusion to the individual because blue is the color of self and orange represents the intention to fuse with an individual's needs. Orange with blue telegraphed FedEx's comprehension of what was needed, which was a predictable, fast way to transport a piece of the self to others.

Use Orange When You . . .

- need cooperation
- want others to commit
- have to incorporate many ideas
- need to let work take priority over personal needs

How Orange Can Enhance Your Work

- If you want to focus on the needs of your clients, drape an orange fabric over an extra chair or use orange file folders to contain papers.
- If you want to enhance the capacity to communicate, glue an orange dot to the most frequently used office communication equipment—fax, printer, copier, or telephone.
- If you find yourself leaving the office frequently, paint the inside of the office door orange.
- If you find yourself daydreaming while staring out a window, hang an orange banner or wind chimes either inside or outside of a window.

Black

The core of black is absence. Black absorbs all colors, and represents the obscuring of light. Alzheimer patients see black as empty space or a hole. An artist knows that black breathes space into a painting and gives the eye a rest before moving on to other lines and colors. And, of course, people wear black to appear less than they actually are. When wearing black, moreover, a person's face stands out and transmits to others' subconscious his or her need for attention.

Children fear creatures in black. Witches traditionally wear black, as do the bad guys in many films. Black can be construed to be an abyss, a hole, or a disguise.

On the other hand, black tends to bring other things into focus. A black sofa with jewel toned pillows or a black cabinet with a vase holding one red rose illustrate the spotlight-effect of black. Black file cabinets are less imposing than light ones and can help office space feel less encumbered.

Lastly, black is associated with the element water and aids in creating calm and reducing anxiety. Just as staring at a body of water soothes us, black in an office setting can reduce jangled nerves and help create a feeling of tranquillity.

Use Black When You . . .

- feel overwhelmed by the number of objects in an office
- want to create a sea of tranquillity around your work space
- don't want your work space to be noticed
- desire others to focus on what you have to say

How Black Can Enhance Your Work

- If you receive clients in a home office and want to distinguish this setting from the rest of the home, position a screen or painting with a great deal of black surrounding your desk's chair.
- If your mind wanders, hang a calendar with a black and white photograph in your line of vision.
- If worry consumes your daily thoughts, paint or cover your desktop in black.
- If you cannot settle down and start working each morning, place black poster board under the workstation's keyboard.

White

Aspiring to be fair, setting high standards, and desiring to impress are the most salient messages communicated by using white in a work setting. By deflecting all colors, a white object is set apart from other items, which incorporates color to blend, camouflage, attract, or repel.

White knights were legendary saviors who by their daring and courageous deeds were distinguished from the common folk. Many cultures use white to imply innocence and purity, including western cultures, which favor females donning white to wed.

My cousin and I recently trekked in the golden triangle area of Thailand with a guide who had been brought up in these mountains. One day when entering a small village, our guide acted particularly frisky and boisterous. We noticed a young woman in white whose flushed face gave her interest in our guide away. Discretion is not the better part of western culture, so to satisfy our curiosity we pestered him until he revealed that this young woman was his intended bride. He had noticed her, in part, because all girls of marrying age wear white until married. How perfect this system is! Parents decide when it would be appropriate for their daughter to marry and fashion a white dress for her to wear. Only then do eligible males consider approaching young women. Thus, when our guide passed through her village, the dress's color signaled her eligibility. White stands out from other colors precisely because it has none.

Physically, by reflecting all colors white is aligned with the metal element. There is a strong reaction to glare that expanses of white can generate. When surrounded by white, a person or an object becomes the center of focus in a more conspicuous way than when encircled by black. Emblematically, white communicates a desire to be in control and the center of attention.

Use White When You . . .

- care to obscure all but you
- desire to underscore honesty and fairness
- need to expose the truth

- want to emphasize your alignment with forthrightness and honesty

How White Can Enhance Your Work
- If you want to be the center of attention, wear white to a meeting.
- If you want to feel in control of your workload, unclutter a white or very light beige desktop.
- If thinking out of the box is a benefit, place a white or clear crystal clock or paper weight on your desktop.
- If mental activity is the mainstay of your job, be sure to have in view at least a three-foot by four-foot area of white on the wall or window at which to gaze.

Purple

While purple is not often used in office decor, some reds and blues that lean toward its hue can be a harbinger of conscious business practices. Ultraviolet light is outside the visible spectrum and cannot be seen; therefore, the color purple is akin to the intangible. Spirituality and the realm of higher consciousness are concepts that are naturally associated with a color that is outside the realm of the readily seen. The royal purple or New Age lavender speaks of purpose, mindfulness, and concerns lying distant from mere survival.

Purple encapsulates humanity's awe of what is beyond physical reality and is an appropriate color to use to capture the appreciation for compassion, empathy, and love. I predict that corporations will increasingly use this color to make their awareness of these global objectives known.

Use Purple When You . . .
- want to communicate global consciousness
- need to set yourself apart

- desire others to come to you when they are wrestling with problems
- are able and willing to assume a great deal of responsibility

How Purple Can Enhance Your Work

- If you want to be more in tune with others' emotions, find a deep purple paper weight for the desktop.
- If you want to boost verbal and written creativity, find a mouse pad or blotter with a purple background.
- If you tend to respond without thinking deeply about your reply, mount a picture with purple in view.
- If you want to feel connected to the purpose and ideology of your product or service, purchase a purple agate to use as a paper weight.

FENG SHUI LAYOUTS FOR HOME OFFICES

There is no ideal setup for an office. What is ideal for one may not work for the next. Evaluate the following suggestions to determine which configuration will serve your best interests to help you thrive at work.

To Focus and Concentrate

- Have visual access to the entrance door, but not a direct view.
- Position yourself to focus on a wall at a distance from your desk. Hang objects that soothe and motivate, such as framed awards, a large plant, or a water feature.
- Do not face a busy street.

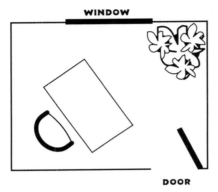

Face a sturdy, imposing, visually appealing object, icon, screen, or plants to concentrate and focus on the tasks at hand.

To Imbue Yourself with Authority and Power

- Position yourself farthest from the entrance door, which is typically to one side on the back wall.

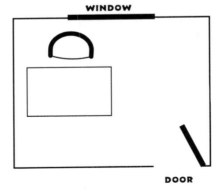

Position your desk slightly off center from the entrance door to command power and authority.

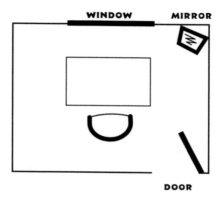

To be inspired, face nature or an enjoyable outdoor scene, but be sure to position a mirror to see the entrance door.

- Place in view any awards or icons of power that you possess.
- Be in view of something that is moving such as a fan, pendulum clock, and the like.

To Be Inspired

- View nature out the window by placing a birdhouse to attract life.
- Hang wind socks, wind chimes, or a flag on brackets inside or outside a window. (Inside, position a fan to stimulate movement.)
- Hang a picture with a natural scene.
- Locate a geode or a water feature on a window ledge or a countertop.

PART III

THE DREAM
ON THE SHELF

13

How to Pick a Winning Business Location

I f work should be like play, and business as usual means tucking your feet into slippers and padding into another room or area of your home, what events could make you want to move into a commercial location? There are only a few good reasons to move a business out of the home.

1. There is absolutely no room to contain all the business material in your home.
2. You find that home life is too distracting to function optimally at work.
3. Customers come to the location on a regular basis.
4. The stimulation and networking of a commercial environment would enhance your business.
5. Your town's zoning prohibits the hiring of employees at home.

When working at home becomes a full-time endeavor, it is time to assign a fully autonomous space to it. When this is not done, a subconscious message undercuts the importance of your work. No one can function at optimum when there are no spatial supports evoking respect and honor. Consider the allocation of space in a typical family home. The more space assigned to a function, the higher in the hierarchy of significance the activity or people assigned to the space is. When a parent's bedroom is bigger than the children's, the message is that parents are more important and in charge. When the family room is larger than the formal living room, it suggests the significance of the family over outsiders.

Even if you live in a small apartment or home and don't have a spare room, look for spaces whose functions are secondary to daily life. In many places the designated dining area is underused. It is often the perfect location to sequester from the rest of the space. A screen, a row of plants, or a sliding wall of shoji screens can separate a small space adequately. Over all, when space is at a premium, you must determine what space is underused and create an ambiance of separation.

If there are no compelling reasons to move from home and your office is overflowing with stuff, it's time to consider allocating additional space. There is no reason why some functions cannot be integrated into other areas of a home. While keeping in mind that the main work area stays separated, look at which functions can be moved. A few suggestions are office supplies, fax and photocopy machines, file cabinets with infrequently used data, and table and chairs for meetings.

Closets and drawers in other rooms are good locations for some of these items. Often they are filled with unnecessary items. My rule is that if I haven't used an item—be it a pot, an article of clothing, or a machine—in a year, then it is probably not integral to my happiness or success. Cleaning out infrequently used things is one way to create space elsewhere for office overflow. Why can't a fax machine be in a closet? Phone jacks can easily be placed inside it. Setting office machinery on a low file cabinet inside a closet can maximize that area's capability.

Attics and basements often have spare areas that can be used for the overflow. It is best to establish office areas near the entrance to these spaces. Be sure to furnish higher wattage in the areas used for office needs. Repeat some details from the main office in the ancillary ones. By choosing the same clock, calendar, or poster, the visual continuity not only connects these divergent office spaces, but also keeps you in the same mental mode when moving throughout them.

When secondary office space is visible in a room, it is important to differentiate it from the rest of the space. An area rug can do the job, as can painting the walls in the area a different color from the rest of the room.

When you outgrow a home office, here are some feng shui rules to assist you in selecting a location that can help your business thrive.

How to Attract Customer Traffic

Our instincts drive us to want to be part of the pack. People are not solitary creatures and are apt to gravitate to a location filled with other shops or businesses. However, specifics regarding the kind of proximity to the heart of activity is critical for success.

I have friends who thought they had struck gold when they found a house to buy on the main shopping street in Woodstock, New York. What they didn't realize until after their first year in business was that it was located one block down the street from the last shop, which meant that foot traffic had to continue past seven or eight private residences before reaching their store. This gap was enough of a deterrent to nullify the location's apparent advantage. The feeling of being in the thick of things is imperative to access, and the public will literally stop in their tracks when the feeling of proximity vanishes.

When selecting a location, be sure to observe the patterns of foot traffic. You'll find that certain side streets are never or are always busy. Also, patterns of use can be influenced by inclement weather, and if your geographic location suffers from a great many rainy, snowy, or foggy days, assess how parking's proximity will affect traffic and accessibility. Sometimes the reason rent is lower in one area is that businesses don't make as much money as they would elsewhere.

Location at a T-Juncture

Classic Chinese feng shui warns us against positioning a build-ing at a T-juncture. A T-juncture causes unusual focus on a location, which is bad for a home but good for business. Con-

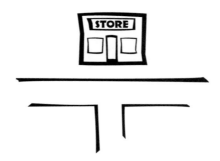

Stores located at T-junctures have more visibility and may be preferred locations.

sider European plazas, which have all roads leading into them. In this case a T-juncture pours people into the plaza. Like a heart, the veins carrying people lead directly to the plaza. A business positioned at a T-juncture will get a lot of attention, and in business we know that's half the battle.

If you are not located at a T-juncture, here are some ways to replicate its benefits by magnifying the entrance:

- Paint the entrance door a bright color.
- Use signage over the door to increase its height.
- Place two plants or columns next to the entrance.
- Install a welcoming outdoor flooring.

A Large or Well-Known Landmark Nearby

Being near a local landmark can be a benefit so long as you capitalize on promoting it. Position your signage and other eye-catching images in the direction of that location. Install an object that moves to catch the eye's attention. If yours is a serious business, a flag will do. If there are no limitations on the public's acceptance, be creative. Any item that responds to wind will do the trick.

Location at a Traffic Signal

Being positioned near an intersection, which stops traffic, can help advertise a business. I always search for things to look at to make waiting for a traffic light to change tolerable. Use ingenuity to entertain, educate, or provide some verbal or nonverbal reason to look in your business's direction.

On the Sunny Side (or Shady Side) of the Street

My one foray into the world of retail was in Newton, New Jersey. We designed a fabulous streetfront presence for this small craft gallery. A five-foot-high papier-mâché face smiled on pedestrians, and the purple window surrounds helped this tiny location stand out like a lighthouse on a starless night. The one problem was that it was located on the shady side of the street, and this town, which sits at the edge of the northeastern snow belt, was bone-chilling cold most of the year. The snow was almost impossible to chip away from the sidewalk, and when the wind ripped down the street, my shady side was eerily empty of pedestrians. For most of the year people traveled on the sunny side of the street, and since my shop was not near a crossing, our side always had fewer customers than those on the other side. Which is needed in your area—sun to quell the chill or shade to protect from a scorching sun? Your success could depend on knowing.

Other Grand-Level Shops

Humans like to be entertained, and window shopping is a form of entertainment. I have observed in my hometown as well as large cities that, given the choice of walking down a street with ground-level shops or walking on a street where the buildings have no eyes on the street, the public's choice is exceedingly clear. Humans pick routes that have visually interesting street-level displays. If you are located in an area where there are no other street-level stores, especially if there is no parking directly in front of the building, you will not accumulate sufficient foot traffic.

FEATURES OF CONVENIENCE

Human beings' natural territorial limits are one-quarter mile or fifteen hundred feet. After that, we feel that a place is a bit too far away to get to and therefore inconvenient. Unless you have a great deal of money to spend consistently to inform the public, or unless special entertainment features are connected with your business, it is in your best interest to make your place of business convenient, such as having sufficient parking closeby.

Accessible Parking Within Half a Block

Although mall shoppers have no problem being separated from their vehicles by great distances this very same group may bypass a downtown location because off-street parking is not adjacent to a business location. In any event, if your business is located in a downtown area, be conscious of how convenient parking is. Stores not adjacent to on- or off-street parking will have far fewer customers.

Safe and Visible Parking

Unless you live in a crime-free area, providing a feeling of safety is essential to building the kind of loyalty that sustains business. Be aware of how customers will likely approach the location, especially if the lion's share of your business is female.

Easy Access Off the Street or Highway

Nothing is more disconcerting than trying to follow sign directions while driving. If the street signs are not utterly comprehensible, new customers may give up or feel frustrated when trying to reach a location. Increasing the size, contrast, and clarity of the signage will help mitigate this potential problem. Contrast is the amount of definition between the letters and the background. Black against white represents the most vivid contrasting colors, while red against yellow is the most noticeable contrast.

Drive and walk by the location from all directions. Does anything block complete visibility? We have all seen road signs that are blocked by spreading foliage and wonder why no one trims it back. If more than two directions are blocked visually, determine how you can rectify the situation.

Questions to Ask to Determine if a Location Is Ideal

Let's imagine a location ideally suited to promote business. What are some important features to consider before signing a lease and investing time and money into your project? By asking the following questions of other merchants, the chamber of commerce, or a real estate broker, you can gather sufficient information to ensure that the location will be ideal.

1. **Has any business failed in this location?** Locating a business in a place where other businesses have failed can dramatically diminish chances for success. If more than one business has failed, the warning is exceedingly clear. In that case only dramatic renovation or changes in the surrounding areas can help a new enterprise succeed where all others have failed. Again, low rent could be a warning.

2. **What are the parking restrictions?** What, if any, parking restrictions are there in the area? If the meter's limitation is one hour, is the shopper rushed? Find out what time attended parking lots close or if the public or employees will feel comfortable arriving or departing during your business hours. Parking regulations can be a guide for business operating hours.

3. **Is public transportation used?** If so is its location convenient? How far away is public transportation? If you have a business from which the employees or customers haul items, consider whether lack of convenient public transportation could limit your employment picture.

4. **Are there restrictions on designing distinctive entrances?** How much control will you have over making the outside entrance compelling and distinctive? Very often what seems like

a minor renovation is blocked by the landlord or county ordinances. Don't assume; check out your ideas carefully.

5. **Does the entrance door swing to the left?** It is far better to have the right side of a door unimpeded. Human beings are right-side dominant, and when entering a building they feel more comfortable moving to the right. Reception areas to the right feel more consumer-friendly than those straight ahead or to the left.

When the majority of the best feng shui is accommodated, the likelihood of a thriving business is enhanced. Far better to pound the pavement searching for the right spot than live trying to remedy problematic conditions.

14

Asking the Right Questions When Designing (or Redesigning) an Office

When it is opportune to rearrange or move to a new office, it's a good time to consider things from a feng shui point of view. Often offices are selected without regard to worker motivation and support of job performance. It's obvious that office workers require adequate storage space, easy access to files, and proper office equipment, plus a desk and a comfortable desk chair. Yet these basics are only the first step. There are many more complexities to consider if you are to transform a mere place into a support for thriving.

Privacy Versus Contact

Consider the following questions before selecting a space or arranging an office area.

Is Privacy a Benefit to the Performance of This Particular Work or Task?

In work that requires risk or creativity, it may be better for a person to feel unobserved. When I was a jeweler, early-morning hours before my assistants arrived would be consumed with what I called *creative play*. I would allow myself the luxury of spending workbench time playing around with materials with nothing in particular as a goal. This creative nonproductivity would eventually serve as an inspiration that would come home to roost in another form. This "nonproductive" time was the seed for growth and ultimately inspired success. Had I worked in a jewelry factory or started work with others by my side, I might not have felt comfortable engaging in creative play since the process was often bumpy and some results were embarrassing.

> Privacy affords the freedom to be experimental.

Is Being Part of a Group Beneficial to the Ongoing Process of This Work?

Would racing records be broken if the athletes ran alone? The energy exuded from runners pounding down a racetrack animates not only the athletes but also those in the stands. In sports arenas, competition provides the impetus to strive for the breakthrough to which athletes aspire. In the workplace, a company's success is often attributed to standards of excellence set by those in charge. When surrounded by dynamic, energetic, optimistic people, it is hard not to feel the same way. In many cases placing the right person in a central, visible place keeps the energy flowing.

My friend is a postal worker who possesses the quintessential New England work ethic. Recently a new supervisor was assigned to her office and morale plummeted. Not only did the new supervisor not do a fair share of the work, but she used the office phone as if it were a private line. Having the wrong person centrally visible may be likened to the one rotten apple and cause the entire barrel to decay. On the other hand, visual contact can be the ingredient that will catapult a team to new heights when the person in charge acts in an exemplary manner.

When Is Partial Privacy a Benefit?

When people are working in the same modality yet responsible for individualized work, partitions separating workstations are appropriate. A newsroom is a good example of a workplace where the actual work doesn't require a great deal of interchange, yet the energy exuded by the group benefits the individual process. Whereas the individual reporter-specific tasks are autonomous, each individual is dependent on the accomplishments and excellence of others to produce the joint results. Newsrooms, graphic art departments, and computer programming companies are some work areas that benefit from this semistructured configuration.

Suggestions for Innovative Partitions

- Mount partitions on wheels for movement.
- Customize partitions by installing a window or opening that allows for direct communication.
- Use lightweight fabric panels on tracks to add movement to partitions, increasing the likelihood of chance movement that will replicate nature's airflow and produce a feeling of well-being.

Make partitions flexible and provide an optional space through which people can communicate while remaining seated

When Should Those in Charge Have an Unimpeded View of Other Workers?

Repetitive tasks can wear down optimum performance. When you can't factor repetition out of a work process, it is beneficial to reinforce positive behavior. Observation by caring monitors can be an impetus to productivity because it is natural to want to shine before someone you respect. Being appreciated can counteract the strain of repetitive tasks.

I practiced piano assiduously when my mother was in the next room. I could picture her pleasure at hearing me play a tune flawlessly. At any age, each one of us wants to shine in the eyes of others. Concentration is greatly enhanced with proximity to a person invested in the outcome.

Physical proximity also makes communication easier. It is not very satisfying to pick up the intercom or use E-mail when asking a co-worker for help, especially if the help involves a cognizant process. The creativity that springs from verbal communication is spontaneous and freewheeling and has an immediate impact. Other forms of communication do not have the cadence and pace of verbal interchange. When striving for excellence, there is no substitute for direct and immediate connection to a positive source for many of us. Corporate consciousness has awakened to the fact that when employees are invested in the final results, productivity and morale rise. Bestowing employees with benefits in direct proportion to business successes is a way of augmenting pride in the whole process, not just their portion of the end result.

Suggestions for Providing Contact Without Compromising Privacy

- Have the office door or office threshold of those in charge placed at a right angle to the general work area.
- Insert opaque glass in the wall above seat level.
- Select flooring that echoes footsteps.
- Mount a bell or other sound device on the office door of the person in charge.

When Is It Wise to Use Valuable Space for a Lunch/Break Room?

Intensity breeds tension and strain and begs for something to counterbalance it. A break or lunch room can be a godsend in businesses involving intense solo work. Water fountains and coffeepots wouldn't be such magnetic gathering places if a break area wasn't needed. Employees deserve a place of nourishment. This room should feel substantially different from other areas in an office to be conducive to relaxation and renewal. Our minds sharpen when we honor our natural biological rhythms. Only at great mental cost can we operate at high gear continuously for eight hours a day, five days a week. A break/lunch room with the following features is essential when work involves many deadlines or time constraints.

Suggestions for Break or Lunch Rooms

- Earth colors on walls and floor communicate a sense of protection and comfort—copper, corn-kernel yellow, toffee, or salmon.

- Upholstered seats, backs, and arms that differ substantially from other office seating can provide the kind of creature comforts normally not associated with work and therefore are balancing.
- Pooled lighting with low-wattage floor or table lamps will furnish a sharply different atmosphere.
- Enveloping the entire room in a comfort fragrance— vanilla or ginger sticks in a basket or spiced apple in a diffuser—contributes to a homey atmosphere.
- Natural sounds—a CD with water sounds or an actual water feature such as a fish tank or fountain—fill silence in a naturally soothing way.

Where Should the Main Activity or Heart of a Business Office Be?

The human body is a fine model for configuring a workplace's physical plant. The heart is located centrally, and our vital fluids return regularly to it. If a workplace does not have a compelling place to which all are drawn, it does not have a heart. When there is no apparent heart or center in the layout of a workplace, it may be best to consider ways of creating one.

Businesses that consume whole floors often have only the elevator bank and a reception area as a common touchstone. Many workers traverse only a small portion of the whole during their workday and have a limited connection to the whole. Humans tend to feel close to those with whom they have daily contact. As in families whose members are spread all over a home or the country, lack of proximity breeds emotional distance.

By selecting a common symbol and repeating it in various locations, you start a visual heartbeat. When I was an artist, clients would often start a conversation by saying something like

"My mother [or aunt] has a piece just like this." At first this approach perplexed and annoyed me, for what artist likes to be told his or her work is not unique? But over the course of years I understood this to be a way of connecting to my art by having it attached to a positive memory. Seeing a familiar icon makes us feel comfortable on a deep emotional level. Therefore, the selection and location of a repetitive element is impor-

Icon	Location
Water feature	Tabletops
Three-dimensional logo	Mounted on walls
Patterned carpet	Under tables
Flag with company symbol	Hung from a dowel from the ceiling
Pictures of four seasons	On walls

tant. Consider these kinds of themes and their locations for the lunch/break area.

How Cost-Effective Is It to Be Stingy with Space?

The coffee machine and water cooler tend to be common gathering places in the office. Impromptu meetings in communal areas tend to renew everyone's enthusiasm for returning to the tasks at hand. Having an alternative undesignated space allows people to test ideas. Make sure that at least 10 percent of office space is undedicated, even if it seems wasteful. Quantum leaps of ideas are less likely to spring forth when there is no non-work-related space.

Suggestions for Getting the Desired Results from Flex Space

RESULTS	SUGGESTIONS
Energy	Water cooler area or negative ion machine
Communication	A white board or chalkboard or surface for push pins
Camaraderie	Two chairs at right angles at a square table
Creativity	A square table for eight people

15

COMPANY IMAGE
AND LOGO

E verything we experience in the world communicates
messages to the subconscious. This means a logo will
be experienced emotionally first, aesthetically second. Feng shui,
the art of understanding how human beings experience all line,
form, and color, can help you determine the impact a logo will
have. Does it project the correct business image? Does the image
match your business's intent, purpose, and mission?

The most important element in your logo is shape, because
you will want to use it in a variety of media and make sure it
is recognizable independent of color. Shape is the container that
delivers the message.

The shape that dominates the logo can be selected from
the lists provided on the following pages. You can most effectively telegraph your message by using the dominant shape that
best corresponds with the image you want to project. To determine if you have accomplished this, squint at the final draft
and see if the shape that represents your field appears clearer
than the others.

Triangle

Triangle shapes capture ideas just as a sail harnesses the wind. For businesses that are innovative, cutting edge, or want to transmit that they confront challenges, triangles are appropriate in the logo. Triangles do not convey a feeling of security and should be avoided in businesses embracing healing, listening, and assisting. Triangles resonate with intellectual processes, not heartfelt ones. A triangle will reinforce your ability to lead and your determination to do whatever it takes to be innovative and progressive.

Professions Likely to Benefit from Triangular Logos

Architect
Aviator
Bodyguard
Detective
Director, theater or film
Legal service provider
Messenger service
Realtor
Surveyor
Travel agent

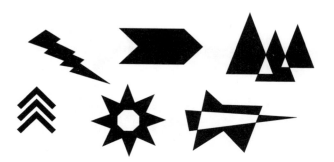

Typist
Tv casting company
Web page designer

Professions That Should Stay Away from Triangular Logos

Baker
Child-care provider
Farming
Human service industry
Naturalist
Personal trainer
Labor relations professional
Property manager
Securities trader

SQUARE

No shape is as sturdy as a square. With all sides or lines the same length, every inch of a square withstands pressure equally. Using the square in a logo design underscores the message of dependability, trustworthiness, stability, and longevity. A business that wants to emphasize its sense of responsibility in meeting schedules can use a square to convey reliability. Professions

involved in building, machinery, or other equipment that wish to incorporate a message of dependability telegraph their commitment by using the square.

Professions Likely to Benefit from Square Logos

Construction
Data entry
Flooring industry
Freelance writer
Housecleaning services
Land developer
Lawyer
Messenger
Proofreader
Psychologist
Secretarial services

Professions That Should Stay Away from Square Logos

Aviator
Motorcycle repairer
Marketer
Hairstylist
Radio announcer or technical support
Fashion designer
Telemarketer
Chiropractor
Electrician
Dancer

CIRCLE

For those involved in the world of ideas, basic scientific research, or other mental processes, applying circular shapes can emphasize the intensity of mental processes. A person who looks at the perimeter line of a circle finds no resting place for the eye. The eye tends to follow a circle's outer line around and around, spiraling mental activity until, like an unraveled ball of yarn, a veritable unending string of ideas is unleashed. A circle connotes ongoing mental activity. If work includes a great deal of thinking and creativity, a circle can represent this splendidly.

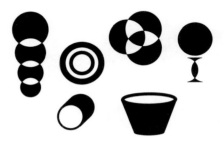

If sorting, selecting, and singling out is part of what your company does, use a circle. A circle, like its elemental association metal, generates a feeling of condensing and straining out extraneous information or matter. If distilling the truth or what's right from a mass of information or being able to spot a trend early is your business, you will find no better medium than circular shapes.

A circle also embraces and enfolds a space. It hugs and protects what is inside as a womb does a fetus. Therefore any design inside a circle will be promoted.

Professions Likely to Benefit from Circular Logos

Architect
Coach
Clothing retailer
Electrician
Interior designer

Jeweler
Attorney or legal secretary
Magician
Marketer
Personnel management
Publicist
Physical therapist
Sales
Security trader
Telemarketer
Typist
Winemaker

Professions That Should Stay Away from Circular Logos

Computer trainer
Naturalist
Nurse
Psychologist
Roofing industry
Seamstress
Home care worker

CURVE

A random free-flowing shape that has no observable repetition is the quintessential representation of a curved line. Experiencing a wavy line is vastly different from experiencing a straight line. Concentration is not necessary to draw a curved line, while it is certainly required to pen a straight one. Curved lines reduce stress and add a brighter, lighter energy to a logo. Caretaking, nurturing, and healing all benefit from a freely-flowing line. If communication skills are a large part of a business's service, the

curved line will give the client a perception of being heard. Curved lines are found more frequently than straight ones in nature, so curves resonate with familiarity and intimacy.

Professions Likely to Benefit from Curved Logos

Ceramist
Cook
Human service provider
Interior designer
Landscape architect
Land developer
Limo service
Hospital personnel
Machinist
Marketing
Commercial artist
Software designer
Textile designer
Nursing and health care services

Professions That Should Stay Away from Curved Logos

Bodyguard
Construction trade

Detective or police industry
Elevator industry
Financial service
Personnel management
Property manager
Security trader
Tv industry

RECTANGLE

Growth, development, and trends are identified with the shape of a rectangle. If a company's bottom line is to expand customers or ideas, this shape is ideal. Expansion, willingness to change, and desire for development are inherently expressed by a rectangle.

The main decision is whether to use it vertically or horizontally. The horizontal rectangle exudes a feeling closely associated with security. A vertical rectangle gives the impression that there is more to come and that this process is one that will be refined and changed as time goes on.

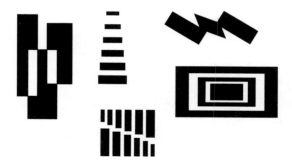

Professions Likely to Benefit from Rectangular Logos

Architect
Travel agent
Chiropractor
Coach
Banker
Attorney or legal services
Marketer
Messenger
Stockbroker or commodity trader
Personal trainer
Publicist
Sales
Typist and secretary
Web page designer

Professions That Should Stay Away from Rectangular Logos

Cancer care industry
Cook
Property manager
Jeweler
Glaziers or glass industry
Nurse
Roofer

Deliver a company's message accurately by carefully choosing the shape that underscores your strengths. When a company's image matches its message, the customer's attention will be fully marshaled.

16

TO LEAVE A
LEGACY

O f all species, only humans have an awareness of death. Because this life process cannot be understood factually, each of us has an unparalleled dilemma to face. Leaving a legacy is one way we choose to give our lives meaning. Since work consumes a great many of our waking hours, it is important to consider how to forge a legacy in the context of work. It doesn't have to be a grand, world-sweeping one, though of course it can be. A legacy unveils to others an exemplary way to act.

Think back to your childhood or any past work experience and consider the people who by their example influenced how you interact today. Each of us carries seeds of those before us who have been a model for our present actions and ways of approaching life situations.

In my childhood, I remember the old grocer who had passed his store on to his son, Rally. Although Rally's dad had retired, he would spend the day sitting near the entrance door, guarding his legacy. No doubt the old man wanted to be sure that his son would not waiver from the standards he had set.

A bell mounted on the front door heralded each customer's arrival. When Rally waited a second or two too long to acknowledge the customer's presence, the old man would shout, "Hey, Sonny, ya got a customer!" When Rally was distracted by another patron, the old man would beckon the customer's children to his side and dig out a piece of candy from the paper bag leaning against the chair leg.

If I was accompanied by my mom, Rally's dad would nod his head as if to say good day and would announce "Missus, Rally got a good leg of lamb today," or some other tidbit equally alluring to our family's palate. Rally and his father knew the eating habits of everyone who entered. When my mom sent me all by myself to pick up meat for dinner, Rally would hand me the brown paper package, assuring me that he had given us my mom's favorite cut. He knew we ate rye bread and dark mustard, and liked herring without cream, and sometimes he would send home a chafing dish filled with his wife's baked eggplant Parmesan. We felt known and cared about, and today's food shopping has never come close to this experience.

Perhaps next to other accomplishments, the grocer's family lesson seems small. However, since my parents were not in the service business, I could not have had a more superlative model to emulate later in life. During those years when I was selling my art, I kept cards on all my patrons, listing their purchases and preferences. I was trying to give them the same individualized service that the grocer's family had given to me and my family.

Think about how your interactions with others can shape their experiences later in life. The influence we generate is not limited to children, for as an adult I am still learning from examples set by people far younger than me.

By using this book's knowledge to recharge and renourish your daily work experience, you bring to the forefront what you esteem about yourself. The more clearly you convey this highest and best form of being, the easier it will be for others to emulate that achievement. Forging a path that others can follow in this way is a legacy that transports your existence into future generations.

A legacy is a gift to the one who gives it as well as those who receive it. By inspiring others, we become their inner voice, which ultimately is heard around the world. By clearing away confusion that chains us to deleterious habits and removing the obstacles that keep us from fulfilling our potential, feng shui helps us reach our heart's desire—a joyful, contented life.

Seize the forces within by dissipating the clutter, confusion, and damaging aspects in your world of work. Obstacles often come in material forms, blocking us from traveling our natural path. In a world where the end is the same as the beginning, what is more important than the joy of the ride?

GUIDELINES FOR DESKTOP CONFIGURATIONS FOR GENERIC OCCUPATIONS

T hese are general guidelines for broad categories of employment. Positions can be altered if you are left-handed or objects added or eliminated depending on specific needs. The templates for each category of occupation is meant to be a beginning point. Just like a shoe ultimately shapes itself to your foot, a desktop arrangement will conform to your needs.

PERSONNEL OR HUMAN SERVICES

You are in the human services industry when most of your time includes meeting and dealing with others.

1. Phone on the nondominant side fosters empathic interactions between you and the client.
2. "In" box in the self-empowerment position indicates that you carry out promises.
3. Pictures of loved ones in the future area confirm a deep commitment to people.

4. A computer on the relationship side indicates the necessity of completing in form what is discussed verbally.
5. Writing implements close by the dominant hand indicate reliability and interest in others.
6. Note pad at right of center or in the self area again underscores your acknowledgment of the importance of the other person.

Data Entry

When the majority of your time is spent entering facts or ideas into a computer, your job can be categorized as data entry.

1. Telephone on the nondominant hand minimizes interest in using this equipment, which can waste valuable time.
2. Writing implements on the nondominant side indicate that writing manually is a second choice. However, the self-empowerment location indicates to others that your assurances are valuable.

3. Note pad located to your left indicates the value you serve to the company.
4. Computer in the future position underscores how important the data is to both your and your company's unfolding success.
5. Because your job has little people involvement, photos or mementos from loved ones are nourishing, positioned in the relationship area of a desktop.
6. Having an "in" box near a dominant hand and located in the compassion position of the ba-gua helps you feel an important part of your company's process.

Sales

If you are involved with creating a demand for a company's ideas, services, or products, sales is the focus of work.

1. The phone and a network resource guide are best positioned close by in the self area. How closely your phone personality replicates your actual presence can be key to pitching ideas successfully.
2. An "in" box filled with qualified leads located in the wisdom segment of the ba-gua can harness the knowing that half the work in selling is accomplished when you have uncovered a good source for leads.

3. A good daily planning system is imperative to a successful salesperson. Locate the piece of equipment that organizes, stores, and informs you of the progress of relationships in the self-empowerment area. In many cases, a computer's software will be a vital source for storing this information.

4. The material you use, whether generated by you or not, is best located in the future section of the ba-gua. The caliber of material is the vehicle representing you and the product. Future sales often depend on an empowered output.

5. Jotting down requests and questions must be effortless; therefore, placing writing implements and note pads close to the dominant hand is essential.

6. Salespeople need support close by to keep their determination and spirits high. Pictures or mementos of loved ones in the compassion area of a desk transmit this support.

Number Cruncher

If you manipulate numbers about half the time each day, then this is your classification. Counting just about anything— dollars, inventory, accounts, materials, or units—is reason to adjust a desktop to this configuration.

1. The center of the desktop, representing financial health, must be clear. For each project, time period, or whatever is the relevant unit in your business must be unimpeded by clutter or reminders of what still needs to be done.
2. Since numbers are not subjective, and what is written often is, place pads and writing implements in the wisdom segment to encourage a measured approach to interpretation.
3. The reckoning or final printout is the product you deliver to a business. Your future depends on how effective your output is. Therefore, placing the printer between the self-empowerment area and the future imbues your work with both power and good prospects for the future.
4. To infuse your work with the human context when you deal with abstractions, keep pictures or mementos of loved ones between the future and relationship corner of a desktop.
5. A computer can be a library of information that can serve decision-making processes. To remind you to use its support as you would a best friend, place it in the relationship area of a desktop.
6. A fax machine in the compassion area reminds you to seek support and keep current.

EDITOR, AGENT, OR PRODUCER

If you work with other people's ideas, are responsible for managing others, or are a synthesizer of talent, this is the desktop configuration to consider.

1. What you have to do and whom you do it with are central to your success. An "in" box and Rolodex are essential tools, and placing them in the wisdom area strengthens your commitment to using them.
2. Your power lies in your mastery for connecting people with people or people with properties. To focus on keeping the stream flowing, place a fax machine in the self-empowerment area.
3. Other pieces of office equipment that keep the flow going are a printer and computer. By positioning them on the power wall and near the future area, you sustain your ability to stay focused and directed.
4. Loved ones or gifts from those you have served are appropriate in the relationship area. The rewards reaped for your talents have benefited others.
5. Using the telephone should be as natural as smiling. Writing implements and pads alongside the telephone make a dynamic threesome in assisting your effectiveness.

Telemarketer

When all your sales are conducted over the telephone, this is your category.

1. There is not a shadow of a doubt that you and the telephone are one. Placing the telephone in the self area is a way of staying focused on the task at hand.
2. The leads and the computer are clearly tools of empowerment. Focusing to the left helps you keep up the energy it takes to communicate effectively all day. Placing the computer in the self-empowerment area can augment your ability to keep up an excellent pace.
3. Live flowers and photos of intimate relationships in the compassion area help balance the rejections consistently experienced by telemarketers.
4. To personalize each contact, place writing implements on the dominant side. You are more effective when you become familiar with those you serve.
5. Pens and pencils can help quell apprehension or drain the stress while on hold or listening to a familiar tirade and waiting to respond. Keep them on your nondominant side in the wisdom area of the ba-gua.

UPPER-LEVEL MANAGEMENT

When you need to communicate clearly and have a positive image, it is best to reign over a clear, unencumbered desktop.

All implements necessary for work should be stored conveniently in desk drawers or nearby, but your face to the world should embody serenity. It is best to have a computer behind or on the side of your operating surface.

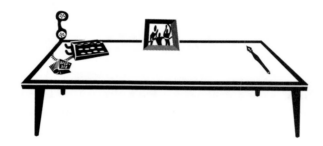

1. A telephone in the self-empowerment area communicates to others that you wield power far beyond the reaches of the immediate establishment.
2. One executive pen should lie in an elegant holder or be set squarely on the nondominant side in either the community or descendant area. This telegraphs the weight of your final approval and increases the care with which others bring information to your attention.
3. Pictures of loved ones in the future area help impart a softer side to this rather austere environment. We are all multidimensional, and placing family photographs in the future area brings a touch of humanity to a business presence.
4. Placing a Rolodex in the wisdom area again clearly sends the message of friends in appropriate places available to you at the flick of your wrist. One of the most impressive executives I ever met kept two gigantic Rolodexes on her desk in plain view of all.

Appendix B

Feng Shui and the Cyber-Office

C yberspace is a strange place, that borderless, intangible zone where E-mail flies back and forth and everything from news to catalogs to music to art somehow makes its magical way from one computer to another. In cyberspace, our senses are virtually null and void, and time and space lose the relationship they have in the natural world. When an E-mail message takes the same amount of time to travel 5,000 miles as 5 feet, and we no longer have to leave our desks to do research, buy materials, or attend a conference, it's no wonder that we lose our grasp of the physical world. This makes today's office a great challenge for feng shui.

To add to the challenge, our digital relationships are fraught with volatile emotions. A recent National Public Radio story reported the various ways people beat up their keyboards, their mouse, mini-towers, and monitors. Feeling frustrated with the most important piece of office equipment of our time is not good feng shui.

My friend Tom Bieschke, owner of the Lyceum Corporation based in Chicago, has adopted feng shui to his computer consulting business, creating what he calls "frustration-free computer zones." Here are Tom's tips for retaining sanity when navigating around a computer's desktop.

1. Do You Like the Way Your Mouse or Keyboard Feels?

Do you own the cheapest mouse or keyboard on the market? Since you are in physical contact with these objects for many hours during the day, spend time shopping for those that fit your hand span and support your movement. Whether or not you can get your company to purchase a new mouse and keyboard, treat yourself to ones with a good fit. Several fine ergonomic devices are currently on the market. If you would not wear the wrong size shoes, you shouldn't use input devices that do not fit.

Recommended products:

- Acer Future Keyboard
- Microsoft Intelimouse Pro
- Wacom Intuos 9″ × 12″
- Logitech Mouse

2. Decorate Your Computer's Foyer

The computer's wallpaper that greets you not only when the computer is turned on but also between changing activities should be as personal and carefully selected as home furnishings. Check out www.digitalblasphemy.com for a Website that offers a vast variety of cutting-edge digital art and choose one that delights you. Choose a background that complements your personality. For example, Tom's water gazebo background balances his metallic personality, and my Space Age odyssey addresses my desire not to let ideas be tethered to the known.

3. Organize Different Tool Bars with All the Programs Needed for Most Commonly Worked-On Tasks

Tired of being interrupted to search for additional programs or files needed to finish a project? In my consultation work I use a word-processing program, a drawing program, a scanning program, and a database program. Tom designed a tool bar for me called "consulting" that, with one click, can bring up all the programs needed for consulting. The new tool bar saves time and aggravation because it's right there with a click of a mouse.

Create custom tool bars for every commonly used program. Start by identifying the most commonly used procedures, then create a tool bar of your own. Almost every new piece of software allows you to design a tool bar that includes those icons used most frequently. Look under the "View" menu. Find "Tool Bars." Choose the "Customize" option and start stealing time away from redundancies.

4. Buy a New Product Only if Your Computer Can Use It Effectively and It Will Produce Faster Results

While this may seem like an obvious tip, hardware manufacturers are making millions on machinery that never gets used, becomes obsolete, and is eventually trashed. Scanners are a great example. If a scanner and the required software are not chosen carefully, the result may be wasted time and money. No matter how inexpensive a product might appear, your time operating the hardware/software is the greatest cost. Like the jackhammer, which can be operated with a trigger switch, eliminating hours of hand hammering, equipment should have advances that clearly outweigh the conventional method. In the case of new technology, it is better to be the last kid on the block to acquire it.

5. Learn How to Fish on the Internet

"I'm lost" is a common feeling we have when trying to navigate through cyberspace. With menus piled up all over the screen and a gray dialogue box in the middle of the screen asking a convoluted question you cannot answer, surfing can be frustrating and dangerous.

So, stop surfing and start fishing. Don't be like those who just throw their line in not really caring if they get a strike. Once you find an area or site that is productive, fish it for all it's worth. Share with friends sites that help you find specific information, fast and efficiently. The following sites are ones I use quite frequently and have helped me snag some "big ones."

1. www.snap.com—my favorite for general information
2. www.mapquest.com—best directions
3. www.expedia.com—best airline fares
4. www.bottomdollar.com—best prices for office equipment
5. www.homescout.com—best real estate search engine
6. www.microsoft.com—best computer software site
7. www.quicken.com/small business—best all-around small business site

One caution: never trust a site for what it rates as the best price or product. Shop around on various sites and talk with real users before making a decision. Common sense needs to be the rule when buying anything through the Internet. Stick to well-known and trusted sites. Always remember you can Ctrl+Alt+Del to end any program or unplug the phone jack to swiftly exit a site that takes you nowhere.

6. LET YOUR VOICE BE HEARD

Adding sound to E-mails, files sent on disks, and interoffice memos can separate your communications from the crowd. Amazingly, everyone (owning Windows 95, 98, and NT) has the capability to send sound bites. The greatest limitation is the hardware of the sender and receiver. Right-click on the "Start" button and choose "Find." Type "Sound Recorder." Look in the C drive. Using this piece of software, you can record CD clips or your own voice. Follow the same procedure to find another program called "Volume Control," or you can double-click on the speaker icon on the tool bar. Use this piece of software to control the input device. Choose "Options," then "Properties," to control the recording and playback devices. Once a file has been created and saved, you can insert it into any E-mail or document.

7. DON'T USE A COMPUTER FOR TASKS THAT YOU ARE COMFORTABLE WITH AND HAVE BEEN SUCCESSFUL WITH VIA ANOTHER FORM

An architect I know once said, "When you can make the computer more efficient than this, I'll use one." He then reached into his breast pocket and pulled out a three-by-five note card and a Cross pen. If you have a system that works, don't change it until you are sure that the advantages will outweigh the original procedure. A computer doesn't have to be used for everything.

Think carefully before you transition from a paper date book to an electronic organizer. A great deal of effort is required to keep an electronic date book current. Consider the difference between flipping a paper date book open, scribbling a change, and shutting the book and doing the same thing with an electronic PIM (personal information manager). First, the computer must be available. Second, the program must be open. Third, the correct spot must be found. Fourth, enter and save the changes. Fifth, close the program and resume work. Busy people may not want to make a commitment on this level for all addresses and appointments. Tom suggests keeping an electronic general schedule and personal information of current clients and a paper appointment/address book for specifics of appointments and an address book that has more permanent/personal/past contacts.

8. CREATE A FAIL-SAFE SYSTEM FOR FNDING FILES

Just like the needle in the haystack, it seems that the smaller something becomes, the harder it is to find. Electronic files are no different and can disappear in a sea of folders, drives, and networks. An easy remedy for this problem is to establish a T.I.P. naming convention for your files. Every time a file is created, a three-part name must be assigned when saved, which can be broken down as follows:

T is for *tool*—tell yourself how the file is being used. Is the file a letter, fax, E-mail, report, presentation, summary, or registry? Look at all of your existing documents and arrive at no more than 10 general uses for all of your files.

I is for *idea*—ask yourself to identify the major thought or point of the file. Is the file an outline, lecture, suggestion, pitch, PR, thank you, follow-up, rejection, or strategy? While your existing files are a good place to find major categories, do not overlook your existing folders. They are a great source for categories.

P is for *people*—identify the individual or group that the file pertains to. Do not hesitate to use both the individual and the group. Many times the only difference between one file and the next is the name of the recipient.

Once you have finished naming the file, save as you have in the past. When you are in need of a particular file, right-click on the "Start" button, choose "Find," type in at least one of the words you used to name your file, choose the drive that contains the file, and press "Find Now." Using this method, you will be able to find any file created. Eliminated is the constant searching through subfolders and the opening and closing of files. Look at the other tabs in the find feature. This simple search engine allows you to find any file by keyword, date, or type of file. By naming your files with the T.I.P. method, the computer is given the power to find files quickly and easily.

9. APPLY THREE MAXIMS TO ALL PROGRAMS

1. *When in doubt, right-click.* Every Windows 95–compliant program has shortcut menus built into the program. Right-clicking produces a shortcut menu of the commonly used features. The right click is like a personal help desk. Right-click on the object in question, and a list of potential answers appears. Choose the option that applies and continue working.

2. *Look for the familiar.* Try to avoid noticing what is different and concentrate on what is known. Don't be distracted by a title: focus on elements you are familiar with, such as the "Minimize," "Restore," and "Close," buttons in the upper right-

hand corner. Most programs have more things in common with each other than are different.

3. *Allow for five minutes of frustration.* I can hear the cry right now, "FIVE MINUTES! I'VE GIVEN THAT MACHINE *YEARS* OF MY LIFE!" Five minutes of constructive problem solving can be more effective than a year of frustration. Don't avoid the "Help" file or "Office Assistant." Start by looking at the suggestions as a hint, not necessarily the answer you expected. Keep asking questions differently, and undoubtedly a coherent answer will emerge.

10. DON'T FORGET TO USE WHAT ALREADY EXISTS IN THE COMPUTER

There is a vast amount of resources in a computer, such as templates few users ever take advantage of. Letters, memos, fax covers, reports, brochures, newsletters, and "whatever" are resting in the "File" menu. By looking at what is offered and even putting needed templates on the new tool bars you will be able to maximize your creativity and not always have to reinvent the wheel that exists inside your computer.

To get the tip of the month, E-mail: the_lyceum@hot mail.com. Remember, feng shui is about space, real or perceived, and employing its principles in cyberspace can make the difference between a comfortable and a disagreeable working environment.

BIBLIOGRAPHY

Beinfield, L.Ac., Harriet, and Korngold, L.Ac., O.M.D., Efrem. *Between Heaven and Earth, A Guide to Chinese Medicine.* New York: Random House, 1991.

Brown, Simon. *Practical Feng Shui.* Lewisville, TX: Sterling Publishing Co., 1998.

Campbell, Don. *The Mozart Effect.* New York: Avon Books, 1997.

David-Neel, Alexandra. *Magic and Mystery in Tibet.* Minneola, NY: Dover Publications, Inc., 1971.

Gallagher, Winifred. *Just the Way You Are.* New York: Random House, 1996.

Hall, Edward T. *The Hidden Dimension.* New York: Doubleday Books, 1966.

Hawking, Stephen W. *A Brief History of Time.* New York: Bantam Books, 1988.

Hendricks, Gay, and Ludeman, Kate. *The Corporate Mystic.* New York: Bantam Books, 1997.

Hunt, Valerie V. *Infinite Mind.* Malibu, CA: Malibu Publishing Company, 1989.

Maslow, Abraham. *Toward a Psychology of Being.* New York: John Wiley & Sons, 1968.

Mojay, Gabriel. *Aromatherapy for Healing the Spirit*. North Pomfret, VT: Gaia Books Ltd., 1996.

Schwartz, Tony, and Wilber, Ken. *A Brief History of Everything*. Boston: Shambhala Publications, Inc., 1996.

Shorris, Earl. *Scenes from Corporate Life, The Politics of Middle Management*. New York: Penguin Books, 1981.

Sinetar, Marsha. *Do What You Love, the Money Will Follow*. New York: Dell Publishing, 1987.

Thomas, Milt. *Common Sense Management*. Fremont, CA: Jain Publishing, 1998.

Wydra, Nancilee. *Designing Your Happiness*. Torrance, CA: Heian International, 1995.

————. *Feng Shui in the Garden*. Lincolnwood, IL: NTC/Contemporary Publishing Group, 1997.

————. *Feng Shui, The Book of Cures*. Lincolnwood, IL: NTC/Contemporary Publishing Group, 1996.

————. *Look Before You Love: Feng Shui Techniques for Revealing Anyone's True Nature*. Lincolnwood, IL: NTC/Contemporary Publishing Group, 1998.

RESOURCES

Tom Bieschke
The Lyceum Corporation
2315 N. 73rd Court
Elmwood Park, IL 60707
Phone: 877-592-3869
Local Phone: 708-583-2120
E-mail: the_lyceum@hotmail.com

The Feng Shui Institute of America
Educational Services & Professional Training
& Conferences
P.O. Box 488
Wabasso, FL 32970
Phone: 888-488-FSIA (3742)
Local Phone: 561-589-9900
Fax: 561-589-1611
E-mail: Windwater8@aol.com
Website: www.windwater.com

Helmet Ziehe
International Institute for Bau-Biology & Ecology
P.O. Box 387
Clearwater, FL 34615
Phone: 727-461-4371
Fax: 727-441-4373
E-mail: bau-biologie@earthlink.net
Website: www.bau-biologieusa.com

I See U
Produce a nondistorting mirror designed to mount
on a computer monitor
Phone: 516-225-1989
E-mail: crisdiseeu@aol.com

John Steele, Aromatic Expert
3949 Longridge Avenue, Suite F
Sherman Oaks, CA 91423
Phone: 818-986-0594
Fax: 818-907-9617

Nancilee Wydra
Founder
Feng Shui Institute of America
Consulting Services
P.O. Box 8001
Vero Beach, FL 32963
Phone: 888-780-7685
Local Phone: 561-388-6106
Fax: 561-589-1611
E-mail: NANCILEEWY@aol.com
Website: efengshuiusa.com
Answers your feng shui questions

Ginny Piech Street
Art for Corporations
Phone: 516-770-2873
Fax: 516-770-4904
E-mail: vstreet@gate.net
Website: www.aaaarrt.com
Creating art for what you need where you need it

INDEX